★ BING
CROSBY
CROONER OF THE CENTURY

Foreword by Kathryn Crosby

By
RICHARD GRUDENS

website: richardgrudens.com

BING CROSBY
CROONER OF THE CENTURY

By
RICHARD GRUDENS

Author of

The Best Damn Trumpet Player

The Song Stars

The Music men

Jukebox Saturday Night

Snootie Little Cutie

Jerry Vale-A Singer's Life

Magic Moments

The Spirit of Bob Hope

CELEBRITY PROFILES PUBLISHING
Box 344 Main Street
Stony Brook, New York 11790-0344
(631) 862-8555

Copyright © 2003 by
Richard Grudens

Published by
Celebrity Profiles Publishing Company
Div. Edison & Kellogg
Box 344 Main Street
Stony Brook, New York 11790-0344
(631) 862-8555
Fax (631) 862-0139
Email: celebpro4@aol.com

Edited by Kristi Watson

Library of Congress Control Number: 2002114476

ISBN:1-57579-248-6

Printed in the United States of America
Pine Hill Press, Inc.
Sioux Falls, SD 57106

Table of Contents

PART TWO
Recalled to Life

PART THREE
People and Things

PART FOUR
The Lists

Sincere good wishes
Bing Crosby

THEME

Where the Blue of the Night
(Meets the Gold of the Day)

Roy Turk, Bing Crosby & Fred E. Ahlert

Why must I live in dreams
Of the days that I used to know?
Why can't I find
Real peace of mind
And return to the long ago
Where the blue of the night
Meets the gold of the day
Someone waits for me
And the gold of her hair
Crowns the blue of her eyes
Like a halo tenderly
If only I could see her,
Oh, how happy I would be!
Where the blue of the night
Meets the gold of the day,
Someone waits for me.

Foreword

Whether or not Bing Crosby is the Crooner of the Century, Richard Grudens is indisputably his chronicler.

The writer's breadth is astonishing. Between the covers of this one volume he has managed to include not only Bing's life and miracles, but also those of every noteworthy vocalist and musician of our time.

Perusing Richard Gruden's manuscript, I learned hundreds of fascinating new details about people whom I've known most of my life. More importantly, I made a number of interesting discoveries about my late husband. Thus I can truly appreciate Richard's talent for research, even though I myself am noticeably lacking in it.

To be sure, I have authored three tomes on Bing, but they were based entirely upon my life with him. What happened elsewhere or previously escaped me entirely. Richard, on the other hand, covers every aspect of Bing's public career.

Viewing Grudens' amazing achievement, I try to console myself with the fact that I wrote of the private Bing whom only I knew, while this book describes everything else.

If we had somehow combined our disparate talents, we could have offered the world a complete description of the Crooner of the Century. In the meantime, I heartily recommend this powerful book to all interested readers.

Kathryn Crosby

Oct. 3, 2002

Bing in *Birth of the Blues*, 1941

Popular SONGS

10¢

BING CROSBY

The Story of
IRVING BERLIN
And Other Features

8 COMPLETE SONGS — WORDS AND MUSIC TO "La Cucaracha"..."Home on the Range"..."Got the Jitters"..."Neighbors"..."Margie"..."You're in My Power"..."After You've Gone"..."I Ain't Got Nobody"

(courtesy Palm Beach Post)

Bing-A Celebration

In the beginning, stiff and rigid sounding popular music consisted of effete Irish tenors singing proudly and loudly and amateurs and black-faced minstrels performing on vaudeville stages, followed by the greatest song belter of all time Al Jolson, who sang out sharply from a stage or runway and directly into the ears of adoring fans.

Then Bing ambled along, fresh from membership in an obscure "jazz" quartet named the Musicaladers, wherein he played the drums and performed vocals, sometimes simply bub-bub-ooing when words were momentarily forgotten, thereby providing the first happy breakaway from the stiff sopranos and baritones of the London and New York stages that dominated all non-classical music. Bing's casual professionalism punctuated the genre with great impact and easy public acceptance because he was an original, a relaxed baritone who was able to embrace and manipulate the revolutionary technology known as the microphone, which he considered to be "...the singer's instrument...." For the following thirty years a parade of performers climbed aboard his ascending star and pursued successful singing careers of their own with a distinct debt to this once-in-a-century personality. Columbo, Como, Sinatra, Martin, Bennett, Tormé, Cole, Haymes, Jeffries, Vale, and more could never have found their own path if Bing hadn't existed. Bing had made a deeper impression on the national culture than any other personality of our time, hence the name Bing Crosby-Crooner of the Century.

Over the years during some of my personal interviews, a number of singers have candidly and openly declared their debt to Bing Crosby:

BING: "It's not difficult to imitate me, because most people who've ever sung in a kitchen quartet or in a shower bath sing like me."

FRANK SINATRA: "He was my hero, the Father of my career. When we in the business are talking about who is best, we put Bing Crosby on a pedestal and fight over who's second."

PERRY COMO: "I tried to sing 'I Surrender, Dear' and 'Temptation' just as he did it back on his 1931 recordings.

Check out my recording of 'Til the End of Time.' It's a perfect Crosby imitation."

TONY BENNETT: "I copied him. No question about it. He made it look and sound so easy. He has actually molded American music."

FRANKIE LAINE: "I used to imitate him perfectly during my Marathon Dancing Days, especially with 'Straight from the Shoulder' and 'Soon'."

NAT "KING" COLE: "Bing once said that he admired me. Well, he called me a real strolling player. Nice words from the master, my vocal mentor, as I once told him."

DICK HAYMES: "Frank copied Bing and I copied Frank — and Bing. Bing was the beginning. Then Frank was next. Perry was there too. I hope I was next in line."

DEAN MARTIN: "If you ever listened to my recordings of 'Wrap Your Troubles in Dreams' and 'Love is Just Around the Corner' you would sue me —if you were Bing Crosby."

PAT BOONE: "Oh, just listen to my recording of 'Love Letters in the Sand' and you will hear my acknowledgment to Bing. He was my stepping stone to success. I am honored when I am ever compared to Bing Crosby."

MEL TORMÉ: "Bing was one of my singing teachers. He encouraged me to sing out."

EDDIE FISHER: "I have always admired Bing Crosby, the great crooner of my youth, from whom I have learned much."

JERRY VALE: "As a kid in the Bronx aspiring to becoming a singer in my own right, I would listen to Bing, Perry, and Frank on my portable phonograph and on the radio. That's how I learned to sing. Bing's recording of 'Far Away Places' alone remains as a solid influence on my career. He and Perry Como were my singing heroes."

AL MARTINO: "As an impressionable youngster, I got started following the sounds of Bing Crosby. I bought his records and listened to him on the radio. He was a definite influence on my career, to say the least."

GUY MITCHELL: "I became a singer when I would listen to Bing sing, and Perry Como too. I could sing well and started out singing like them until I developed my own style of voice."

HERB JEFFRIES: "Are you kidding? I was the black version of Bing, and could imitate him to a 'T'. Bing was my strongest influence. I can still detect him in my work today. When I sang for Ellington, he admired the way I could sing like Bing." [Before he hired a singer for his band, Duke Ellington vowed not to hire one until he found one that sounded like Bing.]

So, why produce a book now about Bing Crosby in the day of mixed, frenetic music, stale and meaningless lyrics, where values are declining and knowledge and recognition of Bing's exemplary musical career is largely unfamiliar to most contemporary music fans?

Well, survivors, performers and fans of Bing's legacy agree that acceptable popular music must be reconstructed and redefined and we, the survivors, will be the catalyst —the organizers who are reinventing, reactivating, and presenting the past through re-issued recorded collections and books like this one. Today's popular music, in the opinion of many, has reached a low point. There is nowhere to travel but upwards. As someone once observed, "There is nothing new under the sun." So we must reinvent our music and insure its proliferation throughout the land once more.

Tony Bennett once declared his career was really never off-track or in decline as some critics have claimed: "There was never a lull. My fans were 'civilized' and faithful during rock & roll's dominating years. I've always performed to sold-out, standing room only audiences, even today."

It may have appeared those performances were held "underground" and not heralded as they once were. Today's performing survivors, Tony Bennett, Jerry Vale, Don Cornell, Jack Jones, Steve Lawrence and Al Martino have weathered the long 50 year storm, now subsiding, and have kept performing, although not recording, and existing on their prolific past glories.

There are an increasing number of radio stations these days filling the airwaves with the music of Bing Crosby's generation. In any given market there are three or four AM and FM radio stations playing Bing's kind of music. There are special one, two and even three hour Bing Crosby, Frank Sinatra, and Perry Como exclusive programs aired on weekends in some markets. There are nationally syndicated programs like Al Ham's "Music of Your Life" and Don Kennedy's Atlanta, Georgia based "Big Band Jump" that specialize in the big bands and vocalists of Bing's period. Veteran D.J. Jack Ellsworth plays Bing Crosby's early recordings every single day on his "Memories in Melody" show on Long Island radio station WALK.

The revival has already begun. On February 27, 2002, the New York Times reported that a fellow named *Beck* downloaded over 8,000 songs onto his computer hard drive, a rotating mix of hundreds on what is known as an iPod, and was listening to recordings by the Beatles, the Rolling Stones' "Stray Cat Blues," the Turtles' "Last Thing I Remember," Joni Mitchell's "All I Want," and remarkably, Bing's 1930s recording of "I Kiss Your Hand Madame," "Mississippi Mud" with Al Rinker and Harry Barris, and "Where the Blue of the Night (Meets the Gold of the Day)," as well as selections by Black Sabbath, Jimi Hendrix, Led Zeppelin, and Simon & Garfunkel.

Holy Smokes!

Let's get Bing's book on the road to back up this regeneration of his kind of music.

Bing's recordings, especially the early ones, make me happy. More folks need to hear them. The world needs cheering up. The world needs Bing Crosby once more.

Richard Grudens
Stonybrook, NY
September 2002

PART ONE

Early Bing
The Road to Greatness

1903. Two Great Entertainers. One, presently established on the East Coast. The other, drawing his first breath of life on the West Coast.

For the first time, blackfaced minstrel man Al Joelson was seen and heard by theater going audiences in a new vaudeville act performed in Brooklyn, New York. The trio of young entertainers Joelson, Palmer and Joelson consisted of Al Joelson, Joe Palmer and Harry Joelson, who presented comedy skits and songs. Limited in size, the words on the theater marquee sign (three names and oval photos of each performer set in-between) needed to be shortened, so the printer omitted the "e" in Joelson to fit in all the names. The wondrous career of *Al Jolson*, later to be recognized as one of the world's great entertainers, was finally launched and would soon be followed by another great entertainer, a crooner by the name of Bing Crosby.

Al Jolson
(R. Grudens collection)

A New Voice at 1112 North J. Street

Some three thousand miles away in Tacoma, Washington, tucked away in a small bedroom at the home of Kate and Harry Crosby at 1112 North 'J' Street, Harry Lillis Crosby was born on May 3rd — a great entertainer's unpretentious introduction to life. The lives and careers of Al Jolson and Bing Crosby were certain to juxtapose somewhere along their roads to greatness in a future generation.

Three days later on May 6, in St. Patrick's church just a few blocks away, baby Crosby was christened, his voice rising vociferously to the celebration. The Crosby family was comprised of seven children: Larry, Everett, Ted, Harry, Jr. (Bing), and later, Catherine, Mary Rose, and Bob; father Harry, an Irish bookkeeper, and mother Kate Harrigan, his strong-willed, talented wife, whose exceptional, clear contralto intonations filled their musical home with sweet songs. She could be heard humming a favorite melody, Johann Strauss' "Merry Widow Waltz," as she gently rocked the children to sleep, even dozing off herself now and then, her head nestled against a pillowed sofa. On the porch of

1112 North J. Street Tacoma. Bing's birth place. *(Ken Twiss collection)*

their modest home, father Crosby strummed his mandolin to entertain the children and introduce his much loved music into their lives. Young Harry Lillis Crosby soaked it all in, as storage for the future.

Young Crosby grew up carefree as a true follower of friends, shy with girls, fast with boys. He loved to participate in sports, especially baseball, and enjoyed listening to music on cylinder recordings his dad turned on the family's Edison gramophone.

BING: "Listening to John Philip Sousa's distinguished band playing 'Stars and Stripes Forever' and the great stuff of John McCormick were wonderful to hear back in those days. We'd all sit around and listen. I think we had the first gramophone in town. My dad explained to my mother, 'We have to have music, Kate,' rationalizing when he spent grocery money on a phonograph.

"Poor mother. She had to make things stretch to feed and clothe all eight of us. She enlisted some neat housekeeping tricks. The laundry was downstairs next to the cellar, where the potatoes were stored. If we kids didn't hang our clothes up, she tossed them down the laundry chute. So there was always a mad dash to retrieve the crumpled garb. We only had one suit for school and another for Sunday."

Just Call Me Bingo

Young Harry acquires the sobriquet "Bing."

"There was a comic strip character in the town's Sunday paper called 'Bingville Bugle' that I enjoyed and would ask someone to read to me, and that's where I picked up the name.

I would sing Bingo, Bingo, and, of course, I loved to sing. So folks started calling me *Bingo*, then shortened it to just *Bing*, and it stuck." His mother didn't like the nickname, which she thought unsuitable for a son whom she thought one day would become a priest.

Bing always performed in school plays. When he was asked to sing, his voice thundered above the rest. He liked singing, but had no interest in memorizing notes or scales, being a typical American boy of his day. He implemented more than his share of scrapes with other kids. Realizing her son displayed possibilities as a singer, Kate Crosby sent him off to a voice coach. Perhaps at one time she would have tried for a musical career herself, had she not married to raise a large family. She thought perhaps Bing could accomplish musically what circumstances denied her: opportunity and chance. Harry showed little interest, wanting no part of it, although he admitted later much regret at his decision to forego vocal lessons and learning to read music for playing baseball.

"I loved sports but had to work for any luxury or entertainment. I wanted athletic equipment and had to get it for myself. That meant work. So I took various jobs. Was once a janitor, peddled newspapers, gathered apples in the summer, anything to finance my needs. My father had a moderate income and could not afford to send us to shows or buy us equipment."

In 1921 Bing completed high school at Gonzaga, a Jesuit school located nearby his Spokane home where the family had moved to from Tacoma when he was six.

Bing's hero was Al Jolson, America's most successful vaudeville entertainer. He was immensely influenced by Jolson, whose songs he heard over and over on the family's cylinder phonograph and later on the new "78" disc recording. The jazzy, exciting music of Jolson and others moved young Crosby along, emotionally arousing his interest and commitment to the craft.

Mentors Harry and Kate Crosby performed regularly in local amateur Gilbert and Sullivan Operettas and always brought home the latest recordings for Bing to hear.

"Gee, Mom," Bing said after catching a moment of his mother's obvious enjoyment while listening to and humming "The Merry Widow Waltz," "You really love the music, don't you?" Bing examined the shellac disc closely, wondering how

Catherine Harrigan Crosby

the infinite number of tiny grooves circling round and round on the disc could effectively recreate beautiful sounds through such a tiny needle.

"My renewed interest in singing, and especially in wanting to perform on a public stage, was mounting day by day. I wound up working in a theatrical prop department whenever traveling vaudeville shows came through town. When Al Jolson's show 'Sinbad the Sailor' came through, as had many other shows from time to time like Willie Howard, Eddie Cantor, Gallagher and Shean, and Fanny Brice, I worked my way to become a theater errand boy and did that several times when Jolson appeared. After listening so often to his recordings, it was strangely thrilling to actually see and hear him sing right in front of you. You know what they say, 'You had to be there.' I found that to be quite true."

At that time, Jolson's greatest song was "Swanee," written directly for him by composer George Gershwin and lyricist Irving Caesar for the long running Broadway show *Sinbad*. Gershwin claimed he had composed the song in fifteen minutes. (It would be 1956 before Bing would eventually record the song with the Buddy Cole Trio). Bing Crosby took what Jolson had done and did it in his own way.

SWANEE
George Gershwin and Irving Caesar

Swanee, how I love you
How I love you
My dear old Swanee
I'd give the world to be
Among the folks in D-I-X-I-Even know
My Mammy's waiting for me
Praying for me
Down by the Swanee
The folks up north will see me no more
When I go to the Swanee shore
I'll be happy! I'll be happy! (spoken)
I love the old folks at home!

"Later, when I got to know and work with Al, he didn't remember me, the lop-eared lad named Crosby who watched his every move, but I remembered him vividly," Bing recalled in his 1953 autobiography, *Call Me Lucky*. "You could never forget Al Jolson. He was absolutely electric. When he stepped onto the stage and started to sing, young and old were immediately captured by him. He was irresistible. Nobody in those days did what he did. The audience just elevated immediately. Within the first eight bars he had them in the palm of his hand."

For a while Bing thought about emulating Jolson, but decided that black face singing was not what he pictured for himself.

*****

The Crosby family became interested in buying an automobile that would allow the family to travel easily around Spokane and even some miles beyond, but the cost wouldn't permit it. Harry's salary, while keeping the family schooled, fed and clothed, was simply not enough.

"I'll get you a Hupmobile, Ma, when I make a million dollars," Bing resolved, "and I will make it some day, you'll share in it. I am going to become a lawyer. They earn lots of money." His mother appreciated her son's ambitious declarations and desires to always help his family. Bing never forgot his promise, which he eventually fulfilled over and over again.

Bing's well grounded academic effort was in elocution, figuring about a time he might dazzle a jury with oratorical mastery. For years Crosby carried around a pocket book size Roget's Thesaurus: "It was fun transposing one word for another. It allowed me to gather up a better vocabulary and sound like I actually knew the language."

Feeling protective of his mother and sisters, Bing would easily became combatant protecting the dignity of Mary Rose, who, because of her chubbiness, was the butt of comments and jokes at her school. Frequently, Bing would engage the antagonist in fiery fisticuffs and became a hero to his sister. But, no angel, Bing would find minor trouble now and then, like the time he and some friends played hooky.

"Once, we became involved in a rhubarb at Jesmer's Bakery, near our house. We lifted some baked goods from an unattended truck, and ran away with some pies and pastries. We ate it all except a few which we tossed at passing motorists down on Mission Boulevard. One car was filled with policemen. We spent the night in the pokey until our moms arrived at the jail the next day."

Then, Bing developed an interest in a pretty young miss at school named Gladys Lemmon. Totally enamored of her cheerfulness and good looks, he would not tolerate any comments, one way or another, concerning his relationship with his love interest. Young Gladys became the defensive chip on his shoulder that others would not try to dislodge or challenge. Bing and Gladys spent time lingering around the phonograph listening to Al Jolson and other present-day musical stars, and Bing thought, "What a great thing, to sing songs and earn money for it."

Very capable at whistling, he would perform melodies he knew while walking home with Gladys, or he would break out and sing "In the Good Old Summertime," or perhaps "When Irish Eyes are Smiling," his rich baritone permeating the air, an introductory event to an inevitable future. It was obvious that young Bing Crosby was musically creative and a natural prodigy, always cheerfully whistling and singing at every chance he got.

Learning at Gonzaga

Among the assemblage of red brick buildings known as Gonzaga University, Bing worked diligently under the Jesuit priests when he entered college, and became a member of the varsity baseball team. The school curriculum emphasized the study of elocution and public speaking, subjects in which he naturally excelled. Bing retained the values learned from these studies throughout his life. But life in a university was much harder work than grade or high school. Through the difficult study of Latin, the challenging intricacies of algebra, as well as continually working at small jobs beyond school hours to earn enough money to keep him going, Bing persevered. Law training in school was drudging to Bing, who privately longed for a career like his hero Al Jolson.

While at Gonzaga Bing organized a quartet that he linked to a band, the Juicy Seven, and played drums and sang. Enamored and anxious to become that Al Jolson style entertainer, he journeyed from school, but was driven back by hunger and for shelter, not unlike his hero's history. There, reunited with his group, Bing would solo on "For Me and My Gal," inadvertently introducing his signature "ba-boo-ing," slipped in when some lyrics were forgotten or misplaced.

The Musicaladers

Mildred Bailey, dubbed the "Rockin' Chair Lady" because of her association with songwriter Hoagy Carmichael's composition "Old Rockin' Chair," was an immensely successful singer when she vocalized with her husband Red Norvo's band.

Excited by Bing's traps playing and vocal ability, Al Rinker, Mildred Bailey's brother, invited Bing to join his band. The group was called the Musicaladers, a six piece school dance combo who played engagements at local restaurants. One roadhouse, Larieda's Pavilion, catered to college kids and featured colored lights and a mirrored ball, transforming the otherwise bleak building into a bona fide dance hall. The boys would play Larieda's three nights each week. Their success catapulted them into the Spokane Theater where they performed their repertoire, developed confidence, and got serious about show business careers. Bing and Al would hang around Bailey's music store in Spokane to learn all the latest songs by listening over and over to the recordings of Paul Whiteman and other Dixieland style bands. Rinker would extract the rhythms of popular recording stars and transpose them into usable collegiate music.

BING: "Al was a genius listening to phonograph records, absorbing their arrangements and committing them to memory by ear. All the Musicaladers operated by ear. None of us could read music. We obviously had no need for sheet music.

"And, we couldn't afford to buy all the records we needed to emulate, so we just memorized what we could listening to the samples of all the new records by the Mound City Blues Blowers and the Memphis Five, sounds like that."

The boys would practice in the basement of Benny Stubeck's Confectionary, a corner lunch counter and candy store. (Bing spoke affectionately about the place, always mentioning it on his subsequent radio shows). Besides rehearsing, the boys spent social time there with girlfriends. Some said they kept the hangout stocked with "moonshine," for all a perfect adolescent hangout.

By this time Bing Crosby was totally infatuated with his music, and began to set aside his keen interest in sports and major studies in law in exchange for a career in music.

Going to L.A.

Checking their progress, Mildred urged her brother and Bing to head South to Los Angeles to try their luck in the myriad of speakeasies that were always searching for new talent. Rinker encouraged and candidly pressed Bing to quit Gonzaga. Bing was earning more money with the Musicaladers than working part time at a law office. Against the advice of Kate Crosby, but with the sly encouragement of Harry Crosby, the two remaining Musicaladers got set to travel to L.A. in a dilapidated Model T Ford they named *Hope Divine* to seek their musical fortune.

Mildred
(Rinker) Bailey

When Kate asked, "How are you going to make a living simply by singing?" Bing replied, "I don't know, but I'm gonna try. Al and I are going to drive down to Los Angeles and try to break into show business, specializing in our way of singing ' hot rhythms.' I probably would have made a poor lawyer, anyway. Al's sister, Mildred, already sings in a band and she's going to show us the ropes. Everett said he would help us financially, if we need it. We will stop off to see him. Don't worry, mom!"

Brother Everett was doing well selling trucks.

"Ma, we gotta try. When I make money, I'll be back to help you and dad."

In a few days they were on their way. Kate packed a lunch for the trip, tearfully permitting her talented son to head for the badlands of glittering Los Angeles in their shabby Ford.

"We broke down over and over. We didn't care, as long as it got us to Hollywood where Mildred and her husband Benny would help us, maybe open a couple of doors."

And open doors they did.

"We're seeing California across the footlights," Bing wrote his mother. They booked an engagement at the Boulevard with a regional group. They liked the life and the camaraderie of the other troupers in show business. They played Santa Barbara, Sacramento, San Francisco, San Diego, and finally landed back in L.A.

"Everyone was in the same pot," wrote Bing.

Bing was entranced by the exciting, pulsating music scene in Los Angeles. Mildred was singing in a plush speakeasy. There was bootleg liquor, fast girls and lots of other kinds of excitement, and, at last, a genuine "gig" — singing for a living.

They christened the act "Crosby and Rinker, Two Boys and a Piano," playing the Tent Cafe, then the Lafayette Cafe in Sacramento, with Al at the piano and Bing scat singing while tapping a cymbal and chopping out rhythms with a drumstick, since they had sold Bing's entire drum set to a service station owner for five dollars cash and 10 gallons of gas to refinance the remaining trip to L.A.

They enthusiastically injected some interesting jazz rhythms into the act, along with some tricky harmonies, and a couple of *boodle-dee-boos* into tin cans, emulating some of Whiteman's leading hits, "I Love You," "Whispering," and "Japanese Sandman."

"We played anywhere we could for any price. We were non-union without a scale — we just took whatever was offered. That's how badly we wanted bookings. Anyway, we didn't need much money to get by in those days."

Crosby & Rinker, 1926

Crosby and Rinker — Two Boys and a Piano

CROSBY & RINKER

Two Boys and a Piano
Singing Songs in Their Own Way

VARIETY REVIEW OCTOBER 6, 1926

NEW ACTS: CROSBY & RINKER
SONGS
Granada, San Francisco

Two boys from Spokane, not new to show business, but new to picture house work. They appeared with Will Morrisey's Music Hall Revue, and were a success in a show that was a flop. Bringing their methods to the Granada, they registered solidly; and on the crowded Sunday performances, practically

Paul Whitemen's Great Orchestra, 1928
(R. Grudens collection)

stopped the show. Wherever the public goes for hot numbers served hot, Crosby and Rinker ought to have an easy time.

Learning to Croon with Paul Whiteman

In April 1926, the boys were hired to play the Metropolitan Theater in a variety show, each earning sixty-five dollars weekly. Variety, the show business tabloid, dubbed them a "success in an unsuccessful show." The amiable, easy-going Bing was always a hit. Their break came when Mildred, now popular and friendly with many important musicians, was able to persuade famous bandleader Paul Whiteman, whose King of Jazz Orchestra was riding the crest of the waves and currently performing at the Million Dollar Theater in L.A., to audition the boys. Whiteman sent two of his best musicians, Matty Malneck and Ray Turner, to check their act. They returned to Whiteman with a *socko* review. Whiteman promptly scheduled an audition that landed Crosby & Rinker a contract for $150.00 a week each for a stunning five years. The former Musicaladers Bing and Al Rinker, beholden to his sister Mildred, could not believe their luck. Now Crosby could warble his heart out and get paid well for it, as was his goal, and with the finest of them all, Paul Whiteman's King of Jazz Orchestra.

All of this made Whiteman more aware of Bailey, whom he subsequently heard singing at a party and, enamored by her engaging vocals, contracted her to become the very first "girl singer" to perform with a touring band. Later, Mildred left the band with Whiteman's vibraphonist, Red Norvo, whom she married. Together they formed their own band to be celebrated as "Mr. & Mrs. Swing."

On October 18, 1926, Bing Crosby cut his very first recording accompanied by Don Clark and his Los Angeles Biltmore Hotel Orchestra, with his partner Al Rinker. The title was popular composer Walter Donaldson's "I've Got the Girl." In the original recording of this peppy ditty, it's impossible to distinguish Bing's voice from Rinker's, although Bing certifies it was indeed him singing.

The boys joyfully caught a train for Chicago to unite with the great Whiteman band at the Tivoli theater to fulfill their *written in heaven* contract.

In Chicago, Paul Whiteman declared from Center Stage:

"I want to introduce two young fellers who have joined our great band. I picked them up in an ice cream parlor in a little town called Walla Walla, and I brought them here to perform for you. [Big jovial smile] They were too good for Walla Walla. [Pause] Meet — Crosby and Rinker."

Al Rinker, with a guitar less strings, and Bing Crosby, holding a French horn he couldn't play, were two enthusiastic players that performed their act to enthusiastic applause.

The Rhythm Boys

It was Paul Whiteman's winning recording of "Whispering" that had earlier enthralled Bing and thoroughly influenced him.

Overwhelmed at his good luck at being associated with Whiteman, young Crosby's dream had been fulfilled.

"I've been very lucky," Bing stated years later. "I started with no particular aim — other than the vague general one of wanting to sing and be in show business. I was seeking no great achievement. I did what I liked most to do. Sing."

The boys were an instant hit everywhere they performed, with the odd exception of an appearance at the New York Paramount where they could not be adequately heard in this very large canyon of a theater, due, they thought, to poor acoustics. Whiteman benched the popular team for the entire New York run.

"We did not know if it was acoustics or bad luck. We did everything the same, but New York audiences let us down. However, it gave us the chance to check out the New York scene. We enjoyed the Cotton Club uptown and had a ball everywhere else. We ran into a feller named Harry Barris, a brash pianist and composer who also sang. We convinced him to join up with us. He did and we re-named ourselves *Paul Whiteman's Rhythm Boys*. We were now a perfectly balanced act."

Enthralled, Whiteman accepted the freshly formed trio, featuring them in every show with his great orchestra. Some of the orchestra's stellar members were arranger Bill Challis; trombonist and clarinetist Tommy and Jimmy Dorsey; cornetist Henry Busse; sax player Frank (Tram) Trumbauer; trombonist Glenn Miller; arranger Ferde' Grofe; trombonist and trumpeter Jack and Charlie Teagarden; cornetist Leon "Bix" Beiderbecke; guitarist Eddie Lang; Vocalist Mildred Bailey; and pianist/arranger Lenny Hayton, all future music legends.

Th Rhythm Boys. L to R: Barris, Crosby and Rinker
(R. Grudens collection)

Aside from performing in New York at just about every important venue in the city, Paul Whiteman's Rhythm Boys undertook an extensive national tour, arranged by Whiteman's agency, the Keith-Albee Circuit, because Whiteman thought the English would not easily accept the new jazz sounds of the Rhythm Boys. The plan had the boys converge with the band in Hollywood upon Whiteman's return from the full-scale tour of England.

In 1927, Bing cut over twenty recordings with Paul Whiteman's Orchestra, including one alone with the Rhythm Boys, "Mississippi Mud," written by member Harry Barris and Jimmy Cavanaugh, and "I Left My Sugar Standing in the Rain." The new combination clicked. With the new and peppy tunes to introduce and perform, the spark was renewed. Hopes were high.

MISSISSIPPI MUD

Jimmy Cavanaugh & Harry Barris

When the sun goes down, the tide goes out
The people gather 'round and they all begin to shout,
Hey! Hey! Uncle Dud,
It's a treat to beat your feet on the Mississippi mud
What a dance do they do
Lordy how I'm tellin' you
They don't need no band
They keep time by clappin' their hand
Just as happy as a cow chewin' on a cud
When the people beat their feet on the Mississippi mud

Arriving in Hollywood, Whiteman announced that the entire organization would be featured in a forthcoming film entitled *The King of Jazz*, in which Bing would perform a solo, "The Song of Dawn." Unluckily, Bing got into a minor scrape with the law involving an automobile accident in which he was not at fault, but nevertheless wound up with a thirty-day sentence because he was flippant to the judge, and, as a result, never got to perform that song in the film.

"My brother Everett came to see me in the jug. He told me that Pops Whiteman had tried to hold my song for me, but when I couldn't be sprung, they gave it to another singer, actor John Boles."

The judge said the citation complaint had included a minor drinking charge. Bing claimed he had a *couple*, but was not impaired. The other driver actually ran into his car. "Although I was certainly guilty of a few youthful indiscretions in those days, once I got those injudicious moments out of my system, I have never let liquor interfere with my work or my capacities."

Bing did appear in the film with the Rhythm Boys and a pre-Andrews Sisters group, the Brox Sisters, performing Barris' bright and tuneful ditty, "A Bench in the Park."

"Actually, 'The Song of Dawn' was not my kind of style. My crooning wouldn't have been very good for that number. I might have flopped with it and been cut out of the picture. It may have been bad for my career."

After the Rhythm Boys' brief appearance in *The King of Jazz*, they were cut loose from the Whiteman organization to embark on their own. Harry Barris had written "I Surrender, Dear," a song perfectly suited to Crosby that would catapult him into the big time, as he interspersed his solo ballads with the bright jazzy patter of the trio. Barris also composed "So the Bluebirds and the Blackbirds Got Together," a ditty that left audiences fractured.

"It was a happy return to our good old days at the Tivoli in Chicago where we first started with Whiteman. Being backed with a remarkable trio, my friends "Bix" Beiderbecke and Jimmy and Tommy Dorsey, we really began to click playing for parties around town, and worked whingdings for other celebrities like the great English star Bea Lillie."

Parting from Whiteman was a significant step for Crosby. Later, Bing would tell the world that Whiteman was kind to him and that he owed a great deal to his former employer and mentor. They parted and remained friends.

On Their Own

After some work at the Montmarte Cafe in Los Angeles, the boys' new agent Leonard Goldstein booked them into the famous Cocoanut Grove, where the *creme de la creme* of celebrities gathered. The house bandleader, Gus Arnheim, signed Crosby, Barris, and Rinker to perform. The shows from the famed Cocoanut Grove would broadcast two hours each night, spreading the boys' musical fame north to radio outlets

Come to the Cocoanut Grove
(R. Grudens collection)

in Tacoma and Portland, Washington and were able to stretch into some Midwest cities.

Gus Arnheim's big band personnel included Shirley Ross, who would later sing a duet "Thanks for the Memory" with Bob Hope in the film *The Big Broadcast of 1938*," and singers Andy Russell, Russ Columbo, and lovely Loyce Whiteman, who later married Harry Barris.

Besides "I Surrender, Dear," Barris composed another of Bing's most successful songs, "Wrap Your Troubles in Dreams," when they performed at the Cocoanut Grove. Both were pivotal to Bing's career. Gus Arnheim's arranger, Jimmie Grier, contributed his fine arrangements of both compositions, greatly enhancing Bing's expanding repertoire. Singers' appearances at the famous Cocoanut Grove were, in those days, a sure stepping stone to success while Arnheim managed the very popular nightclub.

Enter Dixie Lee

She was blond, beautiful, famous, and smitten with the young crooner named Bing.

One night during an engagement at the Cocoanut Grove, Bing's friend Dick Keene, a Fox studio actor, strolled in with a beautiful young blond. Bing took careful note. After the show, he introduced her to Bing, whose smitten heart began racing.

Her name: Dixie Lee.

Dixie Lee, originally Wilma Wyatt, an actress who hailed from Tennessee, had grown up in Chicago. There, she won a singing contest sponsored by the popular blues style singer Ruth Etting (her tag song, "Love Me or Leave Me") and a part in a Broadway musical, and emigrated to Hollywood to be developed into a full-fledged film star by the studio. Dixie and Bing were soon a steady twosome. Dixie's friends tried to discourage her from going around with the irresponsible Bing Crosby, claiming: "He'll never be able to support you. Stay away from this guy!"

Bing had acquired a reputation for arriving late and sometimes actually not showing up at some Grove performances, which caused Gus Arnheim to substitute Russ Columbo as the band's singer. Although Bing enjoyed performing, he was alternately carefree and somewhat emotionally detached, placing more importance on the wanton and wild life, and was

more delighted at catching acts of other performers than he was concerned about his own show business advancement at the Cocoanut Grove. He arrived at area shows with a girl on each arm, ready for a sociable evening.

More well-known at this point, Dixie, in fact, earned more in her movie career than Bing did, causing him to experience noticeable insecurity: "I'd be known as Mr. Lee if I married Dixie," he told his partner Al Rinker, "but I need to become responsible, so marrying Dixie might be good for me."

Bing proposed to Dixie over a plate of fried chicken. Dixie savored the concept of marriage with Bing, but made him promise he would become serious, knuckle down, and she would quit her job, which, the world learned later, was because she was uncomfortable in front of the camera or an audience. It would be a relief for her to settle down as a wife and, hopefully, a mother.

Bing and Dixie Lee tied the knot on September 29, 1930. Bing kept his promises, becoming more responsible and a serious performer, setting aside those playboy-style activities forever.

BING: "I know her family thought I was just marrying Dixie to attach myself to her career, because of who she was. But I was just a crooner working down there at the Grove in L.A. with the Rhythm Boys and had no hope and no aspirations other than that."

DIXIE ON BING: "Fame and fortune didn't make him conceited, careless, or reckless. He takes them as a grave responsibility, a trust to be executed, a burden to be borne, almost like a heritage that he must administer carefully and well."

Dixie Lee Crosby

Russ Columbo

Ruggerio de Rudolph Columbo began his rise to popularity subbing for Bing Crosby, who was the featured vocalist at the Cocoanut Grove when they were both members of the Gus Arnheim Orchestra. Arnheim would call upon Russ Columbo, as he was known professionally, to replace Bing when Bing was late or didn't show up for his performance.

Columbo was five years younger than Crosby and started out as violinist for the band, but caught on as vocalist. Within a few months both he and Bing had their own competing radio programs. Russ performed on NBC and Bing on CBS. Ironically, both shows were scheduled on the same night and at the same time, inviting radio and newspaper columnists to inquire whether or not they were different people. One columnist wryly inquired, "Are Bing Crosby and Russ Columbo one and the same?"

On October 7, 1931, the Hollywood Reporter noted:

"Russ Columbo, former understudy of Bing Crosby in California, is a radio sensation in the East. While Columbo is cutting his wide swath, Crosby is beginning to fade."

Russ Columbo
1930s
(R. Grudens collection)

Newspaper reporters dreamed up a feud, but none existed. The singers actually admired and praised one another, and Russ was a guest at Bing's first son's christening. Bing, although usually one to avoid such events, eventually even became a pallbearer at Russ Columbo's funeral.

There was some resemblance in their voices, delivery, and choices of material. Bing, however, performed brighter, lighter, richer, and more livelier — and at times, outright jazzy. Columbo's approach was more morose and sadder sounding. He blatantly imitated Bing and learned from watching him manage tricks on the microphone, using what he witnessed to his advantage. To most observers there was no mistake as to who was superior. It was clearly Bing. Both recorded

"Prisoner of Love," "Out of Nowhere," "Sweet and Lovely," "Paradise," "Goodnight Sweetheart," and "Where the Blue of the Night," all being among the most popular songs of the moment. It was Columbo who composed "Prisoner of Love."

Columbo appeared in a number of films through 1934. Tragically, on September 2, 1934, Russ Columbo perished when a photographer friend struck a match on the barrel of an ancient pistol. Unbeknown to anyone, there was a shot and powder in the barrel, which fired. It ricocheted off a table and struck Columbo in the head. He was only twenty-six. Would he have become a star as big as Bing? Would that have eclipsed, or even toned down, Bing's stunning career? While Bing's sparkling, but sometimes laid-back, personality was as vital to his career as his voice, Russ Columbo had sold a lot of records and had been under contract to Universal Pictures.

Another similar singer, Buddy Clark, also sang with Gus Arnheim in 1936, closely following Columbo and Crosby. Clark possessed promise, but he, too, died accidentally in a plane crash returning to Hollywood on a flight from San Francisco after attending a baseball game in 1949. He recorded Crosby-style tunes like "June in January," "Red Sails in the Sunset," and "With Every Breath I Take" in the early to mid thirties, as well as a couple of neat duets with Doris Day, "Baby, It's Cold Outside," and "Love Somebody." His most popular recording was Jack Lawrence's song "Linda" written for Linda McCartney when she was a child.

The Sennett Shorts

While performing at the Cocoanut Grove, Bing had had some run-ins with Grove manager Abe Frank, who withheld pay from Crosby because he sometimes arrived late for appearances and even skipped a few. However, one afternoon Bing was approached on a golf course by filmmaker Mack Sennett, who offered him a chance to make a series of film shorts. Lucky Bing signed with Sennett, and just in time.

The story of Sennett's discovery of Bing goes like this:

Willie Low was the head pro at Lakeside Golf Club in Hollywood, and was interviewed for the Club's 50th Anniversary wherein he revealed that Paul Whiteman had a number of golfers in the band at the time he made The King of

Jazz in 1929. Bing and Al Rinker were his best golfers. In the fall of 1930, Low was giving Sennett a golf lesson. Bing was playing alone and caught up with them on the second hole. Low noticed Bing's approach and asked Sennett if he minded Bing joining them. He didn't know who Bing was: "I told Sennett Bing was all the rage at the Cocoanut Grove, and that all the women there were wild about him. Sennett said, 'Bing, Willie Low tells me you sing.' Bing replied, 'Yes, they call me a crooner,' and Sennett asked him over to the studio. That's how it happened. I know because I was there."

"Sure, Abe Frank docked my wages and he was within his rights. But, I was able to defy him being encouraged by my Sennett contract, so I quit. Working in movies was easy money. Abe Frank also placed a union ban on my singing in those film shorts because he was pretty mad. Sennett got around it by using a pipe organ or a ukulele or an *a-cappella* (without live musical instruments) choir in the background. Or we simply

worked to canned music, which meant I sang to a recording played on a phonograph."

The production of Sennett film shorts was simple and direct. Sennett's genius, of course, had previously produced the former successful *Keystone Cops* films. The cast of these two-reel shorts gathered in and around Sennett's office and plotted each story that always concluded with a treasury of physical vaudeville gags and Bing getting the girl. A signature Crosby song always wrapped up the film, with the entire cast beaming.

The Sennett films were all produced between 1931 through 1933 and lasted about twenty cute, romantic, and funny minutes. One take for each scene was usually enough. It kept the budget down and permitted a two-day shooting schedule per film. Most were produced outdoors in the Hollywood Hills. They were, chronologically:

I Surrender, Dear	(released Sep.13, 1931)
One More Chance	(released Nov. 15, 1931)
Dreamhouse	(released Jan. 17, 1932)
Billboard Girl	(released Mar. 20, 1932)
Blue of the Night	(released Jan. 6, 1933)
Sing, Bing, Sing	(released Mar 24, 1933)

When young Bing Crosby appeared in the Sennett shorts, he was musically fresh and uncorrupted. Fast becoming endeared to millions, Bing's Sennett films helped jump-start his prolific singing career, never since equaled by any other singer. Crooning "Auf Wiedersehen," Bing's hand gestures and charming facial expressions, which were emotional, sincere, and unlike any vocalist before him, were typical in all the shorts and further established him as an actor, although his acting then may have appeared to be clumsy due to corny story lines. It was obviously Bing's crooning that made the films successful, establishing a brand new face with a brand new voice and a brand new approach by showcasing Bing's singing talents on film.

BING: "Well, the best thing about the Mack Sennett shorts, and I made a bunch of them for both Sennett and the Christie Brothers, was the training it gave me in adlibbing. They never had much of a script. You were just told to go into a scene and adlib some dialogue with the other characters, and when

Sennett dropped his handkerchief, you made an exit. That taught me to be resourceful. I had the opportunity to work with a lot of good gag men and I think it was great training."

On the Radio

Duke Ellington, after hearing Bing sing, vowed not to hire a male vocalist until he found one who sounded like Crosby.

With all this going on, brother Everett Crosby quit his job as a truck salesman, deciding that being Bing's manager would be a more desirable way to earn a living. Bing sorely needed his services. Bing could sing, but could not manage. One of Everett's important chores, contacting CBS Radio in New York and pitching Bing for a show based on his Brunswick recording successes, became the important vehicle and Everett's prize for Bing's career.

....

Bing & the Boswells.

....

Ironically, CBS chief William Paley happened to be returning to New York on a steamer from Europe a few weeks earlier. On board, a youngster in an adjoining deck chair kept playing Bing's recordings of "Just One More Chance" and "I Surrender, Dear" over and over on a portable gramophone. The tunes, and the unconventional way they were delivered, captured Paley's interest in this new-style singer. He asked the young man if he could read the platter. To Paley, the sound of Crosby was indeed different, and he needed a different kind of singer to perk up his rating-sagging early evening radio programs. He brought the information back to his New York office and dispatched underlings to search for the singer with the odd name of *Bing* Crosby.

Coincidentally just days later, Paley, in his office listening to Everett's submitted air check audition of Bing singing, literally leaped from his chair shrieking with the realization that his prize was at hand. "That's him! That's the guy I told you all about that I heard on the ship... the singer I asked you to find," he shouted to CBS's talent department executives gathered there in the boardroom. "Call Everett Crosby!"

Everett was promptly summoned to New York, and Bing subsequently signed a CBS contract at $600.00 a week, with promises of more to come if a sponsor signed on. "I have often wondered what would have happened to my career if brother Everett had remained in Tacoma selling trucks," Bing recalled.

Extensive publicity was launched for Bing's nightly series of fifteen minute programs at a prime time, seven o'clock, coast-to-coast network spot. Ironically, Bing lost his voice before airtime because he was anxious and had over-rehearsed for four solid hours, postponing the widely publicized premier three times. The fourth try was at last successful, and with his pal, guitarist Eddie Lang, accompanying him, Bing crooned Paley's favorite, "Just One More Chance." Bing was perspiring profusely, and by the time he worked through the first few bars, he knew his vocal chords were back on track. Eddie Lang winked, and Bing, now bubbling with confidence, let his voice cry out his songs full force.

JUST ONE MORE CHANCE
Sam Coslow and Arthur Johnston

We spend our lives in groping for happiness,
I found it once, and tossed it aside.
I've paid for it with hours of loneliness,
I've nothing to hide,
I'd bury my pride for
Just one more chance
To prove it's you alone I care for
Each night I say a little pray'r for
Just one more chance.
Just one more night,
To taste the kisses that enchant me,
I'd want no others if you'd grant me
Just one more chance
I've learned the meaning of repentance;
Now you're the jury at my trial.
I know that I should serve my sentence,
Still I'm hoping all the while you'll give me
Just one more word.
I said that I was glad to start out,
But now I'm back to cry my heart out
For just one more chance.

Instinctively, through trial and error, Bing effectively learned the use of the newly developed microphone. He discovered how truly intimate and effective individualistic microphone singing could be, having a knack for gathering elements of jazz from pioneers he knew into his own easy style, including "scat" singing, a technique he borrowed from his friend Louis Armstrong. Bing's offerings possessed rhythm and flawless phrasing. His voice and the microphone were actually Bing's *musical instruments* just as sure as Benny Goodman's clarinet and Harry James' trumpet were theirs.

Bing's success story took fast flight. Singing on radio inspired an exciting and contagious fever among listeners from coast-to-coast. Bing's career had caught fire. Fans wrote and wired the studios, local and national. CBS slipped other performers into the show: The Boswell Sisters, Kate Smith, and Morton Downey, all well-known performers, were added. Sheet music and records of Bing's repertoire sold in unprece-

dented quantities. Just about everybody was listening to the relaxing, easy going singer Bing Crosby. Brother Everett haggled with would-be sponsors, demanding pie-in-the-sky compensation to allow their products to be marketed on Bing's show. A cigar manufacturer, Certified Cremo, became Bing's first sponsor. Bing became a very popular radio property.

Bing at CBS
Radio, 1930s
*(R. Grudens
collection)*

Over the next few years, the fast developing days of live radio entertainment, Bing continued to emote songs of the moment, regularly appearing with many of the leading entertainers of the day. He collaborated on and introduced "Where the Blue of the Night (Meets the Gold of the Day)" and retained it as his theme for his entire career, as Bob Hope kept "Thanks for the Memory." Bing's charm and breezy style on radio captured the public's imagination, retaining superiority for over 20 years. Bing enjoyed radio. He would wear his flamboyant style sport shirts (Bing was colorblind), a Tyrolean hat to hide his baldness, and spend most of the show perched on a high kitchen stool, while humming to himself. He chewed gum like crazy and rolled it under his tongue when he started to sing. After each show he was usually the first one out of the studio, hurrying to the parking lot, hopping in his car and taking off before autograph seekers could get to him.

In 1933, Chesterfield Cigarettes sponsored Bing. Woodbury Soap took a turn in late 1933, paying Bing's bills through 1935. *The Kraft Music Hall* lasted eleven beautiful years through 1946 emanating from NBC in Hollywood. Bing's famous *Philco Radio Time* show, an ABC program on-the-air from 1946 until 1949, was followed by Chesterfield Cigarettes return sponsorship (1949-1952), but this time Hollywood hosted, on CBS once again.

General Electric renewed sponsorship on CBS from 1949 through 1952. During a portion of 1952 through 1954, various sponsors signed checks for the *Bing Crosby Show* through 1956, and *The Ford Road Show*, from CBS in Los Angeles, was a subsequent, happy two year showcase. Bing's long-running radio programs wound down with the *Bing Crosby-Rosemary Clooney Show* on CBS in L.A., concluding in 1962 after a two year run.

All in the Family
Everett, Larry and Pop Crosby

Bing Crosby wisely had his father and brothers manage his business and financial affairs, but brother Bob Crosby was an added yarn.

*****

At the time when Bing Crosby's brother Everett convinced Bing to travel to New York from Hollywood, where he was filming the Sennett shorts, to sign a radio contract with CBS, he decided to set up an office in Bing's dressing room at Paramount. Everett named the new company "Bing Crosby Ltd., Inc." He soon supervised the purchase of a six year old, three story building on the Sunset Strip for $80,000.00 which was mainly occupied by the Crosbys, but seldom frequented by Bing himself.

Everett and Pop Crosby at the office. *(courtesy LOOK Magazine)*

When Bing didn't care about being listed for star billing in a movie, Everett would always fight for it, but Bing, never an egotist, wanted no part of self-importance. He always believed others in his films were equally entitled to an even break because he val-

ued the help they contributed. Everett finally backed off and allowed Bing's wishes to be met.

"A special clause was inserted into all Bing's contracts that stipulated that two stars must appear in every Crosby picture," said Everett in an interview, "and that Bing could never be starred alone without our consent. The two stars line was eventually dropped, but the part that they couldn't star Bing alone still held. You will never see Bing Crosby starring 'alone' in any film."

For Bing, Everett was the ideal manager, a man who was willing to shamelessly bicker with radio and film executives to obtain better deals for him, no matter what or how long it took, something Bing himself could never have achieved, even for his own benefit. It just wasn't in laid-back Bing to argue contracts or demand higher fees by exchanging shouts or tousling with agencies, producers, sponsors, and advertising people. Everett, a very powerful manager, was known in the trade as either *Dr. No.* or *The Wrong Crosby*. He was the keeper of the keys to Bing Crosby. If you wanted to hire Bing, you had to talk to Everett first. He was involved in the acquisition of all Bing Crosby commercial byproducts, from his interest in the Pittsburgh Pirates baseball team to his shares in Minute Maid Frozen orange juice.

Everett was the only Crosby who resided in style in Beverly Hills, collecting first edition books, old paintings, antiques, oriental rugs, and, as Bing used to quip, "good food and rare wines, too!"

Brother Larry Crosby, formerly an advertising man in Seattle, joined Everett in the family enterprise, to become Bing's public relations director, working on special projects like Bing's Golf Tournaments and Army Camp entertainments, of which there were many. He would usually say, "Everett makes the deals, and I take care of the details." Larry also handled all fan mail, which at the time equaled more than all other Paramount players combined!

Did they ever have arguments? Larry would grin and say, "Well, yes we do! Us Crosbys are very opinionated people."

Larry, a practical utilitarian, grew an orchard behind his house in the Toluca Lake region where he raised chickens, ducks, goats, and turkeys. It was said that Larry would pay his son twenty-five cents to feed the chickens but had to chase him all over the neighborhood to get him to do it. The brothers named Bing's mansion with its majestically colonial designed columns and circular driveway "The Toluca Lake Library."

Bob (top),
Bing, &
Everett

Bing's father, known to one and all as *Pop Crosby*, worked with Larry and Everett. A lifelong accountant, Pop handled finances and served as liaison officer between the office and Bing. Pop Crosby had another assignment as the daily courier. Bing, forever carrying his office with him, often had to be tracked down, so Pop drove around looking for him at all his haunts, including the golf course or his home. When he located Bing, he would hand him checks to sign, letters or contracts

Crosby Inc.
1930s. Los
Angeles, CA
*(courtesy LOOK
Magazine)*

to approve or disapprove, and memorandums from Larry or Everett. Bing reviewed them, issued some instructions, signed checks, letters or contracts and placed all in a large envelope. In the morning, Pop picked up the envelope from Bing's house, only eight blocks from the house Bing purchased for him and his mother, and brought them to the office. The Crosby clan were an enthusiastic, cohesive team who labored lovingly on Bing's behalf. The Crosby business was a family affair.

Despite the closeness of the family, something odd regarding Everett's grave site was noticed by Bill Hunt of the *Bingthings Society* in 1995. Bill, who was involved with many Crosby projects, searched for the grave of Everett Crosby in the hills of Northwestern Connecticut: "It's one thing to be gone, it's another thing to be gone and left alone. Bing has a whole tribe of Crosbys buried around his gravesite, but Everett was buried alone. His widow re-married and moved away so the grave was not visited much. Bing's and Kathryn's son, Harry, lived not too far down the road. However, I was enthralled by the natural beauty of the setting, but I kinda wish he had more Crosbys around him."

Bob Crosby

George Robert Crosby was the last born of the Crosby kids, and became best known as the suave bandleader of a great Dixieland Band. He gained his fame in the 1930s and passed away in 1993, the last survivor of the seven Crosby children. His band was a rollicking, swinging band of eight players, much like those that Benny Goodman employed within his own band. Bob tried to differentiate himself from his famous brother. He could sing, but his low confidence and efforts to compete with Bing placed a shadow over such a career.

When Bob Crosby had graduated from Gonzaga University, Bing was already world famous. Bob started his career with the Anson Weeks Orchestra, and later tried out with Tommy Dorsey as a band singer, but it didn't work out. Bob didn't enjoy hearing the phrase "Bing Crosby's brother, Bob" when he got up to sing. His range was the same as Bing's, but he conscientiously sang in his own fashion. When Bob appeared at the Palomar Ballroom right after Benny Goodman, Bing loyally made a personal appearance as a send-off.

Frequently overshadowed by Bing, Bob would brood, sulk, and sometimes even lose his temper when someone compared him to

his brother, not that it was anyone's fault. As a result of this behavior, he acquired a reputation in the business for being an introvert.

....
Brunswick
Promo
(R. Grudens collection)
....

For some people the adjustment to the fame of a brother or sister is a serious and common, yet little recognized, problem. As Bob once explained, "One symptom of this *brother complex*, if I am any true barometer, is that adult victims tend to behave like asinine juveniles. Once, for instance, my band, the Bobcats, was booked to play a dance hall in the South. We were greeted by a large sign the dance-hall owner had thrown together. 'Tonight, See the Bobcats, Led by Bing Crosby's Brother.' I charged into the impresario's office, spitting mayhem. 'Get rid of that sign or I'll quit now,' I screamed. Shocked, he asked, 'What's the matter? Aren't you Bing's brother?' I didn't answer, just slammed out the door. The Bobcats pulled me off an outgoing train, then got the promoter to rip down the sign, even though he insisted it would cut the box-office take by $1,500.00. As if in retribution, he vanished with the payroll when our booking was up."

It would gall the life of Bob Crosby to have people seek him out after a show just to see if Bing had come to visit or to

ask him to mail them Bing's picture. The same thing occurred on golf courses. But Bing never got any jobs for Bob, never opened important doors, never advised on bookings, and rarely came to see him perform.

"I didn't realize he was doing me a favor and that he wanted me to gain the self-confidence and the enduring success that comes when you build it yourself, brick by brick. By then I had lost all my confidence. The word in the industry was that the junior Crosby was no senior Crosby. I tried my luck on Broadway and everywhere. So I chose to become a bandleader instead. I didn't want to be accused of riding on Bing's coattails. Bing was a better singer, but I was going to top him at something. So I formed the Bobcats, and over the next seven years, we were jazz-mad gypsies, roaming the country to play dance halls, picnics, carnivals, and cabarets with great success."

Bob Crosby organized an elite band of Dixieland players and clicked with audiences on radio and at hotels and ballrooms. In his frantic effort not to be like his brother, he consciously altered his natural singing style. Bob's fellow Marines were the ones who finally got him back on track. Bob became a Marine at the outset of World War II, leading a jazz band in the Pacific war zone. As a lieutenant, and with no USO shows around, Bob performed with a new batch of Bobcats. Someone in the Marines once told him, "Hey, Bob! You're holding back when you perform. I can tell. You know, you're almost as good as Bing, and that's smash-hitting in any league."

So, at the next show, Bob's opening line was, "Hi — I'm Bob Crosby. I'm the one without *Hope*." Then he poured out quips about Bing. "I sang loud and clear and did hundreds of shows like that with the new confidence I acquired."

Bob realized the value of that Marine's expression and accepted it with pride. He became warmer and stopped fighting his mental phobias and scarecrows. He was finally winning the small war over himself while he was fighting World War II in the Pacific.

When he arrived home after the war, his wife June, who had suffered along with Bob for many years, noticed Bob's positive adjustment. She encouraged him to reorganize the Bobcats, but this time with a leader who had no intention of trying to be another Bing. The results were terrific, and bookings came in droves, so much so that a CBS executive who heard the show one night signed him as the singing star and emcee of the *Club 15* radio show. With that success confidently in hand, the great comedian Jack Benny signed him as a radio show regular and CBS further placed him in charge of his own TV show five afternoons a week and sometimes had him sub for singer Perry Como.

"I became the *lucky* Crosby." Bob went on to help others who complained of a brother, sister, or father complex, stating, "Don't trade on your kin's reputation, but don't crawl into a hole either. Learn to accept the relationship and others will end up judging you for yourself, which is what your goal should be."

He told them not to be in any contest with their famous or successful relative, and to stop worrying about finishing second or even third.

"It doesn't matter if you don't do as well materially — all you want is to be happy in your own chosen way."

Bing's Hawaiian Legacy

BING: "It seems every time I visit my friends in Hawaii, I return to the Mainland with the haunting strains of their love-

(Paramount)

ly music lingering in my heart. Months after I've been home, I can get misty-eyed just by hearing any of their beautiful old standards again."

Bing has always been directly associated with Hawaiian music. A few seasons before achieving worldwide fame, and long before the days of wide-body jets and high-rise hotels, Bing heard the first pure strains of the music he would come to love so much and which would consume much of his efforts and interests, the lovely sounds of the lyrical music of the Hawaiian Islands.

While on a holiday in Honolulu in 1935 with Dixie Lee at his side, Bing was visiting an old friend, Harry Owens, whom he worked with in Los Angeles during their developing years when Harry was a bandleader at the old Lafayette Cafe. Harry had since gained popularity as a respected composer and leader of the Royal Hawaiian Hotel Orchestra at the famous Royal Hawaiian Hotel on Waikiki.

Here, Bing first heard a beautiful song his friend had composed about his own baby girl, Leilani. It was called "Sweet Leilani," which meant *Flower of Heaven*. Harry played it nightly as his signature tune. Bing was captivated by this gentle Hawaiian ballad and sorely wanted to include it in a new movie he was about to start shooting in L.A., *Waikiki Wedding*, then in preparation at Paramount Studios.

Harry Owens was not favorable towards allowing the song to leave its natural and original environment, to be cast out into the world where he thought it would be diluted and perhaps diminished in value — even if it meant extra money. Somehow, Bing was able to convince Owens to allow him to offer the song to Arthur Hornblow, the film's producer. Hornblow had some very successful movie hits behind him and knew what he wanted, always getting his way. And, in any case, Bing remembered he was a difficult man to win over.

"I knew a spot in the script where the song would fit in," said Bing, who was not one to put off either, "but Hornblow said there was no chance, that they had all the songs they needed."

When the picture started and they came to the scene where Bing wanted the song placed, Bing said: "I raised the matter again with him and once more he said no. So, I went off to the

golf course! I said to him, 'When you change your mind, I'll be back.'"

Eventually convinced, Hornblow placed the song in the movie. It and the picture were international successes, captivating audiences everywhere and going on to win the 1937 Academy Award and become Bing's first gold record.

Four other songs in the film were "Blue Hawaii," a charming, romantic ballad; "In a Little Hula Heaven," a cute archetypical boy-meets-girl ditty of the thirties; a lesser-known tune entitled "Okolehao" that Bing never recorded commercially; and another which he did, "Sweet is the Word for You."

The film was played out by actual Hawaiians and not Hollywood extras (besides the main characters) and Bing's clothing was typical Hawaiian shorts a yachtsman's cap, occasionally a T shirt with a denim jacket, and a large share of leis like the genuine Hawaiians wore. This translated into the dis-

tinctive Hawaiian flavor that Bing fostered and then mirrored to the entire world. He would be seen wearing Hawaiian style shirts and hats everywhere he went, from the golf course to the racetrack, and in recording and radio studios, well into the forties and fifties, always sporting that casual, nonchalant image that defined his personality, and which he credited to the allusion of life he experienced in the Hawaiian Islands.

Bing became the foremost interpreter of Hawaiian tunes on the Mainland and for many years hence. You could hear this music regularly on his popular radio shows: "Moon of Manakoora," "Mele Kalikimaka" with the Andrews Sisters, "Lovely Hula Hands," and "My Isle of Golden Dreams," which he sometimes said was his favorite song of all. Bing sang songs of Hawaiian character better and more often than any other Mainland performer!

In retrospect, it would be safe to say that in 1937 the Hawaiian Islands were generally little-known and out of reach for the average vacationing citizen in the then 48 states, especially considering the condition of the crumpled economy that prevailed just after the Great Depression of 1929.

Bing, through the escapement of his Hollywood films, his albums, and individual recordings, helped focus attention on the faraway, romantic Islands of Hawaii and helped motivate interest in the average American's consciousness for that future dream vacation trip to the most beautiful state in the Union, Hawaii.

SWEET LEILANI
Harry Owens

Sweet Leilani, Heavenly Flower,
Nature fashioned roses kiss'd with dew,
And then she placed them in a bower,
It was the start of you
Sweet Leilani, Heavenly Flower
I dreamed of paradise for two.
You are my paradise completed
You are my dream come true
Sweet Leilani, Heavenly Flower
Tropic skies are jealous as they shine,
I think they're jealous of your blue eyes,
Jealous because you're mine
Sweet Leilani, Heavenly Flower,
I dreamed of paradise for two
You are my paradise completed,
You are my dream come true.

The Del Mar Turf Club

Bob Hope calls a race track a horse-drawn vacuum cleaner.

Mother Kate Crosby did not work in Bing's business as her husband and children did. She was more interested in horse racing, especially since her son Bing was President of the grand Del Mar Race Track. Employees and other individuals associated with Bing would slip her hot tips which she played and mostly lost. Bing would try to give her tips, but she always lost.

A serious Catholic, Mother Kate Crosby frowned upon her son's drinking, smoking and swearing. Not even one drink would she condone. Her sons tried to compare her playing the horses to their having a drink or smoking a cigarette, but to no avail. However, she was happy that her son Bing helped develop the beautiful track and was able to involve much of his family in the enterprise.

Bing, who had dreamed about such a project, always harbored a fascination for horses and horse racing. With his brother Larry as financial manager, the Del Mar Turf Club was built on acreage located near the Pacific Ocean between Los Angeles and San Diego, California, not far from his own limited Rancho Santa Fe stables. Del Mar was organized in 1936, and constructed in 1937. Its California mission-style buildings dominated the turf.

Bing had to come up with three hundred thousand dollars, not an easy chore considering it was smack in the middle of the Great Depression. It wound up costing over one half million. Bing employed help from well-known actor Pat O'Brien, a horse lover who starred in the successful film *Knute Rockne — All American*.

"I was an eager participant with Bing," explained O'Brien.

Bing and Pat O'Brien at Del Mar 1937

"He was President and I was Vice President. On opening day, we hadn't finished painting the place, and hardly anyone showed up anyway. Soon we we able to attract fellow actors Jimmy Cagney, Clark Gable, and Spencer Tracy — guys like that."

"It didn't look good for us," Bing said, "until a few weeks later when we started attracting a few punters."

They named the track Del Mar. Bing implemented the slogan "Where the Surf Meets the Turf," coined by his friend Midge Polesie, and created a song co-written by Johnny Burke, Jimmy Monaco, and himself, as a theme that was played at the track for many years thereafter:

BING: "There's some talk going round near and far I've heard from good authentic sources, the picture shows me and my horses. On my right, and on my left, stand celebrities. Wait, I'll see if they feel up to par. I'd like to call on just a few to have them sing a word or two, 'Where the Surf Meets the Turf at Del Mar.'"

MARY MARTIN: "From now on my 'daddy' doesn't count, My heart belongs to Paramount, Oh, where the Surf Meets the Turf at Del Mar"

PAT O'BRIEN: "It makes you laugh, it makes you cry, and yet the Irish never lie, 'Where the Surf Meets the Turf at Del Mar.'"

BING: "Business began to pick up. Along came the *Tinsel Town* celebrities and their seekers. Every Saturday night the *creme de la creme* showed. The parties were terrific and lasted to three in the morning. Mary Martin would get up and do something. These were the best fun days."

To further arouse interest and promote attendance, Bing called upon Bob Hope for help. They recreated some of their old vaudeville routines, leaving some to think about the possibility of a Hope-Crosby film venture.

Bing got NBC to broadcast a half-hour radio program from Del Mar on Saturday mornings. Bing and his announcer, Ken Carpenter, would wander about the grounds interviewing patrons and asking them trick questions. Then Bing would sing a tune or two.

Bing had bought his first horse in 1935, naming it Zombie, calling horses in general "slow coaches." He loved to help train and clock his horses around the track. Unlike most horse owners, Bing was always at ease with horse trainers and track personnel. He liked the smell of the racetrack and the action horses brought. His first horse ran at Santa Anita (California) Racetrack. At the time of Del Mar, Bing owned thirty horses and ran seven in one season. Some friends swore he was more interested in horses than singing or making movies.

Bing found it frustrating to try and place bets at the betting windows because fans would swamp him, so others had to place his bets. One of his own horses won the first race at Del Mar.

As a further note, the legendary horse Seabiscuit won a race at Del Mar, as they say, by a "nose," beating out one of Bing's own.

"For me it was a treasured memory, even though my horse Ligaroti lost. It was a photo finish. But to see two fine horses put on such a performance was worth anybody's money. When the chance came for me to get out, not only with the money I'd put in but with a small profit, I sold my interest.

"To me, a race track is for people who can afford to lose a little and are reconciled to losing money they won't miss. Over the years I've met hundreds of horse-players, players who knew every angle — even with access — but the percentage eats up the players and you eventually lose. Go to the races, but go because you love the sport; don't go to make money. It can't be done."

In 1943, Del Mar race track, which operated from 1937 to 1941, was converted into an airplane parts manufacturing feeder plant for the war effort.

Life with Dixie Lee

Blame it on show business, but Bing traveled a lot during their marriage and Dixie Lee seemed lost without him. While Bing was away Dixie frequently sent letters to wherever he was because she missed him so much and had to let him know:

> Bing Darling,
> Your letters are so wonderful. I wish I could be like you —gee, you're lucky — and write long letters. It was so funny — I called Carroll Carroll (Bing's writer) to give him your phone number and Bo said he was talking to you. It makes it seem you're so near. If I could only give you one kiss, I'd let you go back again. I went to the Ice Follies with Alice (Faye — wife of Phil Harris) and Hugh last night. They were very good. Having read this one I'd like to tear it up but you said even hello and good-bye helped, so here goes.
>   I love you — I love you
>   I love you — so there—
>   Dixie

> Angel,
> Don't laugh when you get Gary's letter — I had nothing to do with his line "Don't fall in love." He said he told you that to save you a "bump on the noggin" and to save my arm from using the rolling pin. You don't suppose he's been reading Jiggs and Maggie [a syndicated comic strip of the time] do you?
> Gee, they're funny kids — they seem so much closer to me than ever before. Maybe I take them for granted when you're here and when you're gone they remind me of you.
> Dixie

> Angel,
> You see what happens — Marge and Charles came in right in the middle of my letter. Got all of yours this morning and was I happy. It just makes me more lonesome for you.
> I'm glad you're getting a nice rest. I didn't realize you weren't feeling well — you never let anyone know, you brat. I'll write more often to make up for not having this at Rio.
> I love you darling with all my heart.
> Dixie

Dixie Lee Crosby never wanted Bing to do anything because of her that interfered with his work. And between them (it seemed to work both ways) Bing would never ask anything of Dixie that she did not want to do or felt uncomfortable about.

According to Bing, as long as it was right, fair, and honest, they each did what they pleased. When Bing went anywhere, it was because she wanted him to go. It was the same with

Dixie. If she wanted to go anywhere, she simply went. Neither went on the theory that marriage was a trap. They married because they were in love and refused to let a family and homes turn their love into a cage.

BING: "She knew I was in show business, as she had been, and that I had to go lots of places other men don't...unless they happened to be in the military or a traveling salesman. That seemed difficult...if not impossible...for many to understand."

When Bing was home he and Dixie were always together. They both enjoyed the running of the horses at either Del Mar or Santa Anita.

Dixie Lee loved the Christmas season, spending months in advance to prepare for gift giving. By October, an entire room was sequestered and stocked with a table and rolls of wrapping paper, tinsel, holly, cards, and paste, preparing for what Bing referred to as Operation Christmas. Dixie never forgot her hundreds of friends acquired over the years and made the Christmas season the time she reached out to all of them. So many gifts were needed that she would press friends and her secretary into service as shoppers. A week before Christmas, the Crosbys went into the local delivery business. Some presents had to be sent overseas for her friends in England, France, Hawaii, and South America.

BING: "I've never seen packages wrapped so beautifully...the colors, the silver balls, the holly and other ornaments. It was a shame to have to open them."

Dixie would stage a surprise party for Bing on his birthday:

BING: "When I left for the studio that morning, all was as usual. Linny was getting ready for school, Dixie was at breakfast, the rest of the family bustled about. When I got home at seven, the Crosby house grounds had been transformed into a tropical garden with a great marquee stretched from the back patio to the end of the lawn. There were tables bearing candles in red and white and palm trees had been planted around the patio which was converted into a huge dance floor. And, at the end of the garden was a bandstand with the full compliment of the great Les Brown orchestra aboard playing 'Happy Birthday.' It was an extraordinarily happy occasion as only Dixie could muster."

The party was held on May 2, 1952.

The First Four Boys

The Los Angeles Times reported: "Hollywood. Oct 17, 1959. Bing Crosby saw his sons' night club act for the first time last night. The singer watched the early show of the four Crosby brothers — Gary, Phillip, Dennis and Lindsay. He laughed and clapped heartily during the performance. Afterward he met with the boys in their dressing room. Gary, the oldest at 26, had been feuding with his father for several months. Gary posed for photographers with his arm around his father."

It was inevitable that the four Crosby boys would try to follow their father into show business. Gary had formed the group, and opened with jokes about his relationship with his father:

"Well, here we are, four boys trying to get ahead without the old man's money," or, "That's the biggest hand we've had since we told dad we were leaving home."

On the Ranch at Elko, Nevada
(R. Grudens collection)

Bing & his boys singing
(R. Grudens collection)

Bing and his boys L to R: Dennis,
Phillip, Lindsay and Gary (top)

Bing with Lindsay
(courtesy K. Crosby)

Bing was very fond of his children. Regardless of business commitments, he headed home and spent as much time with them as possible. He developed them rough — at — play, saying they had to learn to "take it". He called them his "Gangbusters," for they were rough and ready kids just like their dad.

Bing would take them to sing at the Hollywood Canteen during the war, and then went around to friends' homes, like Rosemary Clooney and Bob Hope's, to have them serenade them with their versions of Christmas carols.

Gary

Gary Crosby and his dad recorded two charming duets: "Sam's Song" and "Play a Simple Melody." An idea of Decca's Jack Kapp, it unexpectedly became the first double-sided gold record in the history of the recording industry, and Bing's 21st. Gary continued to record a series of albums and singles with Warner Brothers, Verve, and Decca, with "You're Nobody 'Til Somebody Loves You" as his best-selling single and "The Happy Bachelor" as his best-selling album.

An accomplished dramatic actor, Gary appeared as a regular cast member on *Adam 12*, the *Bill Dana Show*, and made guest appearances on *Dragnet, Emergency*, the *Twilight Zone*, the *Dick Powell Theater* and *Murder, She Wrote*. He appeared on Ed Sullivan's TV show, *The Colgate Comedy Hour*, and has performed with Jackie Gleason, Perry Como, Bob Hope, Jack Benny, and toured as a featured vocalist with Les Brown's Band of Renown.

One of Gary's own shows, *Big Band '94*, was built around talking about and performing songs written by songwriters that visited his mom and dad when he lived at home. Among them were Johnny Mercer, Hoagy Carmichael, and Phil Harris. Gary opened that portion of the show, performed with the Pied Pipers and the Guy Lombardo Orchestra, led by Al Pierson, at the Ambassador in Pasadena, California, where he sang a full repertoire of songs. The few references to Bing were neither laudatory or negative. Unfortunately, or fortunately, depending of your perspective, Gary's success was attributable to his father's. Accepting Gary and expressing applause by many was a tribute to Bing himself. Gary may have been offended, and as a result, became his own worst enemy due unfairly to things beyond his control.

When Gary began to write his infamous autobiography that ultimately trashed his father, the other boys promptly spoke up to famed columnist James Bacon to counter Gary's charges that their father was extremely strict and downright cruel. Gary had always been a problem to his parents. Although he and his brothers spent each summer wrangling horses and punching cattle at the Elko Ranch when he was young, something any boy would consider a remarkable experience, Gary stated he hated those days, because, as he complained: "I had to be there." His brothers did not have that problem, according to Phillip. All who knew Bing rejected Gary's accusations, including a close friend, bandleader Phil Harris: "I never heard of any abuses by Bing on his boys. I loved Bing and his boys."

Barbara Crosby (Gary's Wife) in 1983

"I do not know if what's in the book that Gary wrote is true but he never said anything to me about whippings. I think it all got a little out of hand. I certainly never witnessed anything between him and his father. I couldn't believe it when I read the book because it just didn't sound like Gary," Barbara said.

According to Phillip in 1998, Gary was a mean, angry, lazy person who would do or say anything to get his way or get out of trouble. "He wanted to become the new Elvis Presley, and if he didn't he was going to blame everybody else, like he always did." Phillip also revealed that Lindsay was somewhat manic depressive, something he thought Bing did not understand.

Bing himself was brought up under a beloved but strict mother who, even when her boys matured, did not allow them to swear or smoke in her presence. That included Bing, no matter how wide his fame. Bing was strict, but always fair. He felt it a duty to protect his four sons from some of the negative consequences of his widespread fame.

Many pundits, critics, tabloids, radio and television news programs, hungry to exploit celebrity notoriety, glamorized Gary's nefarious book, "Going My Own Way," written with Ross Firestone, further extending the unfair damage to Bing's otherwise exemplary reputation created by its publication.

Apparently Gary's editors had encouraged him to trash the relationship with his father by exaggerating reality in order to sell more books. Gary later retracted his invalid complaints, but the blasphemous damage provided a lasting negative effect.

Situating the boys every summer on his over 25,000 acre cattle ranch where they mowed and stacked hay, repaired fences, drove cattle, and were paid only one dollar a day, Bing believed he was properly developing them, forming a favorable, constructive work ethic while simultaneously protecting the boys by distancing them from the Hollywood and L.A. scene. Bing had them up at 5 A.M. and to bed by 9 p.m. and kept it that way.

Bing's insistence on the right to live his life with his wife and children outside the fan magazines justified his rigidity when it came to protecting his family. An exemplary actor, shunning sexual content in his films, who went about his business, kept his private life as reclusive as possible.

Gary was also a problem for his parents upon entering college: "The biggest mistake I've ever made with my boys was giving Gary a car as a high school graduation present.

"When the Dean at Stanford replied to me upon inquiring of Gary's progress, saying 'Don't worry about how Gary is doing, because he won't be here after Christmas,' the red flag went up and Gary and I had a serious talk. As a result the car was sequestered in a garage until Gary turned academics around. Dixie was even more angry than I concerning his disinterest in his studies versus riding around campus in his new car."

Dixie would remonstrate Bing for not being strict enough. He was either Captain Bligh in a Hawaiian sport shirt or a cream puff who would take his kids to a movie ten minutes following a punishment. "Bing, you punish them then take them to a movie. That's bad," said Dixie. "You should allow the memory of a punishment to linger so they'll remember it. Like the time they took my canary out of its cage and you fanned their rear, then took them out for ice cream because you felt guilty." Bing was fair, and gave up the lickings when they got too big, then grounding or calling off baseball games or locking up the TV for a few days.

On the other hand, over the years, Bing was noted for demanding his kids and old friends to participate in his movies in one way or another over objections of movie moguls, directors and producers. When his boys were 12, 11, 11, and 7, Bing had them appear in the film *Out of This World*, and were each paid $12,500.00 for holding their noses while actor Eddie Bracken moved his lips — and Bing's voice came forth. It was Bing's method of seeing more of the boys by permitting them to interact with him in his work.

Phillip and Dennis, the Twins

Phillip Lang, (Yes, there are two L's in this Phillip) named after Eddie Lang, Bing's late best friend and guitar accompanist, and Dennis Michael, named after Bing's mother's father, were born on July 13, 1934.

"I never realized how famous my father was until he won the Academy Award in 1944 for *Going My Way*. We knew he sang, but not for a living, thinking he only sang at home for enjoyment. He would sing all the time, even in the shower. I remember the Oscar event from the newspaper headlines. The house was just chaotic with calls and telegrams. All the kids at school knew about it, and I remember thinking, 'My God! I'm really proud of my old man. He's really done something great.' We weren't ourselves after that — we were *Bing Crosby's kids*."

For the boys it became a stigma of sorts. Other kids would threaten to beat them up for no valid reason. Once, at school, Phillip was punched in the nose, the kid declaring, "I just wanted to see what it would be like to hit Bing Crosby's kid." So Philip smashed him back most soundly. Each of the boys had to defend themselves in various situations while in school, and, like their dad, were always ready to ably defend themselves.

Dennis earned quite a name for himself performing in local amateur rodeos while dealing with his "hard life" during summers as a rancher, but grew tired of it when girls and having fun came into focus as he grew older.

"Phillip and I said there must be something other than cows. Dad also wanted Linny to become a priest. So I said, 'Dad, I don't think Lin's quite made out to be a priest,' I implored him, so dad gave up the idea."

Phil and Dennis attended Washington State College at Pullman to study animal husbandry, thinking they would become more involved in the ranch. They, however, were called into the Army, which dampened and distanced them away from their original intentions.

But Bing would always be there for them all, and was always giving his boys a helping hand when they asked for it.

"I was a disc jockey at ABC radio in Los Angeles. The other boys were just getting out of the Army. Gary got us together and started to push us to get together and form an act. Dad kind of stayed in the background and said, 'If you want to do it, go ahead, that's fine with me.' But he never pushed us."

The boys enjoyed about four years of success. They squabbled a bit, however, and found their names in the papers if they misbehaved or got into fights when drinking. Dennis married Pat Sheehan, a Las Vegas show girl, and Phillip married show girl Sandra Drummond. Both ladies performed in the chorus at the Tropicana Hotel. When engagements become fewer and needed income dried up, the boys split up and went their own ways. Comparisons with their father proved sometimes fatal. They could have handled it better, but they didn't.

....

Bing and his first family *(R. Grudens collection)*

....

PHILLIP: "I know there is no disguise I could wear to cover up the fact that Bing Crosby was my dad. I certainly am his son. So, I never took him out of the act. I talked about him; I

used him; I used him a lot in comedy; I bounced off him. Its very well meant and I do sing some of his hit records, which are well received. But that's about as far as I go; I don't try to imitate him anymore than that."

Phillip was fortunate to travel with Bob Hope's USO troupe overseas entertaining servicemen in 1967, (his second trip,) performing with Raquel Welch and Barbara McNair, doing some crooning and standup routines. He loved Bob Hope, whom he'd known since his youth. He also appeared in Frank Sinatra's film *None But the Brave*.

Phillip in 1999

"About Gary and his book 'Going My Own Way:' Gary was being interviewed on television and I couldn't believe my ears — he was trying to build a case for child abuse. My parents were strict but they weren't overstrict. My Dad was not the monster my lying brother said he was. He never beat us black and blue and Gary was a vicious, no-good liar for saying so. I have nothing but fond memories of dad, going to the studios with him, family vacations at our cabin in Idaho, boating and fishing with him. To my dying day, I'll hate Gary for dragging Dad's name through the mud. He wrote that book out of greed. He wanted to make money and knew that humiliating our father and blackening his name was the only way he could do it. He knew it would generate a lot of publicity and that was the only way he could get his ugly, no-talent face on television and in the papers. My dad was my hero. I loved him very much, and he loved all of us too, including Gary. He was a great father."

Phillip is the one remaining Crosby son from Bing and Dixie Lee. He has been married three times, has four children (one, Brian, perished in a motorcycle accident), and six grandchildren. He lives close to his daughter Dixie Lee and her two children.

Dennis eventually stopped performing and found an interest in the sound equipment business.

Lindsay

They say Lindsay, born on January 5, 1938, and the youngest of the Crosby boys, was much more protected by Bing.

"We were very proud, but we led normal lives and when I look back I know how tough his schedules must have been. Yet, he always made time for us, especially me as I got older. The other boys went away to school, and I was the youngest, so I was the only one around and he started me playing golf. I took a real liking to it then; I know he gave up a lot of his time to play with me. I think, probably, I never realized how big he was until my early teens."

In 1951, when Bing was the nation's leading recording artist, all of his boys appeared with him on "A Crosby Christmas," a medley of James Van Heusen and Johnny Burke songs. That year it sold 600,000 records. Not bad for a singing dad and his four backup singing boys.

BING: "You know, I don't claim any prize as a parent. I know I overlooked things I should have taken care of. But, it was difficult since I was on the road a lot as demanded by my job as an entertainer.

"I think I failed them by giving them too much work and discipline, too much money and too little time and attention. But their mother and I did our very best."

Bing set up a trust for the boys, which Phil still enjoys today. When they appeared on his radio shows or for any other venture, they got paid but never saw the check. The checks went directly into a trust fund which was managed by Bing's attorney, Jack O'Melveny, who also administered Bing's investments and financial dealings successfully for many years. To Bing, a young person could not appreciate money that was simply handed to them without doing anything to earn it, a throwback from his own youth of always working hard to provide for his own needs.

When Bing moved into the San Francisco Bay area the boys only saw him when he visited Hollywood for television shows or when they called upon him at his Hillsborough home.

It's fair to state that Bing did his best for Gary, always helping him to achieve contracts and instructed his business manager to find work for Gary when he needed help. Gary was never really was able to prove himself as a capable performer. He was always abusive and indulgent in his relationships, and drank heavily requiring professional help paid for by Bing and Kathryn. J.Roger Osterholm, in his book *Bing Crosby-A Bio-Bibliography*, stated succinctly, "Gary began to realize (later) that for years he had been maintaining the hostilities (between him and his father) all by himself."

On June 18, 1952, Dixie Lee had exploratory surgery. The pathologist found terminal ovarian cancer. She remained in the hospital until June 25. She died on November 1st at 9:50 PM. Dixie was only forty-one. Some 600 members of the film colony attended the services at the Church of the Good Shepherd in Beverly Hills, California. Bing was near collapse, holding tightly onto his son Dennis' shoulder.

Dixie bequeathed her half share of Bing's fortune to her immediate family with half going to Bing's mother, her father, her stepmother and her husband. The remaining half went to her four sons in trust. Gary was 19, the twins, Phillip and Dennis, 18, and Lindsay, 14. The inheritance tax on the estate was so high that Bing sold sixty-five race horses to help raise the one million dollars to pay the taxes. According to the New York Times on July 22, 1953, "Under California law half of a husband's property legally belonged to his wife and on her death must pay inheritance tax on that part of the property she willed to him."

BING: "I will never talk about my grief at losing her. I believe that grief is the most private emotion a human being can have, and I'm going to keep mine that way.

"But in the years ahead I'm going to sorely miss her love, her steadfast and constructive support. Dixie was the most completely honest person I've ever known, and the most courageous. Two weeks before she was gone, she took daily transfusions to build up her strength so she could come to the station and meet the train that brought me home.

"And she was there just as she'd always been: beautifully dressed and smiling. I don't ever want anything more in life than the memory of all she did for me."

Bing — Strictly Business

Newsweek April 12, 1948
THE ROAD TO RICHES: Bing Crosby and Bob Hope have made a strike in the West Texas Oil fields. They're partners of W.A. Moncrief Sr. of Fort Worth in the discovery of flush production in the North Synder pool in Scurry County. Millionaire Hope phoned the news to millionaire Crosby: "Congratulations, Bing, you are now a millionaire."

The Minute Maid Orange Juice Story

Bing regularly invested in various ventures. He once owned stock in Decca Records but when he cashed in, it was a great loss. His investments in Minute Maid frozen orange juice were successful, as were his investments in oil fields with Bob Hope. In 1948, when Bing owned 20,000 shares at ten cents a share of Minute Maid Orange Juice, one of the first companies to market frozen orange juice, the company had just acquired an additional 4,700 acres of orange and grapefruit groves near its three processing plants in Florida. The price of these newly acquired properties was five million dollars.

Bing was introduced to the idea of purchasing Minute Maid stock by legendary capitalist John Hay Whitney on a Long Island golf course. Where else? By the 18th hole, Bing had agreed to buy shares of the Vacuum Foods Company product, parent company of Minute Maid, dominated by "Jock" Whitney. Bing became a director of Vacuum Foods, then signed to plug the product on radio under an agreement with the Philco Corporation, which had Bing under exclusive contract.

For Bing, the orange juice business outlook was bright, and the chances for long-range profit for his investment looked even better. "Jock" Whitney always had shown a talent for choosing and financing winners. As we know, Minute Maid concentrated, then froze the juice. When packaged, opened, and mixed with three parts of water, the frozen juice became,

Selling Orange Juice
(K. Crosby collection)

at that time, the closest possible product to fresh squeezed juice.

Minute Maid moved into the field in 1945 at a processing plant in Plymouth, Florida. There was limited cash to advertise, so it lost over 450 thousand dollars in the first two seasons. "This orange juice thing is the wonder of the grocery world," said Vacuum President John M. Fox.

When it "turned the corner" the demand became greater than any produce product in 50 years. Shipments to distributors had to be allocated. Crosby suggested setting up a California plant.

Bird's Eye and Snow Crop, among others, began to produce their own concentrate. Profits soared, and Bing made *lots of money* on his investment. His radio promotions lifted the demand even higher. Bing became the Pied Piper of orange juice, luring customers away from the old accepted brand names.

In the beginning, Minute Maid's initial success came when it proved that frozen orange juice could have a fresh squeezed taste. When Bing boosted the product, his ten cents a share increased to $14.75 a share (paper profit was $293,000.00). His radio plugs on a song and talk show program five days a week worked very well for him and his stock. At this time Minute Maid orange juice was selling 213 million cans of juice per year.

In January 1956, the New York Times reported the Minute Maid Corporation became the first new stock admitted to trading on the New York Stock Exchange in the new year. Bing had been a director but now the President of the Bing Crosby-Minute Maid Corporation, which was the West Coast distributor for its products. Bing bought the first one hundred shares, wiring the order from Los Angeles and then turning the shares over to the library fund of his alma mater, Gonzaga University.

When the closing gong sounded, the tallies showed that 8,700 shares in all had changed hands with the final price $18.25 a share. Apparently, show business was not the only business that Bing could succeed in.

Here is a Minute Maid Minute on radio from Bing Crosby
Good morning from the ranch of Crosby
Plenty of chores around here before breakfast
and the chief rancher, that's me

Bing sells Philco
(R. Grudens collection)

Bing and Audio Tape

When Bing appeared on the Kraft Music Hall Radio show, he asked the sponsor and NBC for money to allow him to pre-record his show on a wax disc. He was turned down. Bing disliked the inconvenience of the late broadcast hours and the necessity of repeating a show for different time zones. So, Bing found a sponsor and network that would allow him to record his show for later broadcast, a first for radio.

The 1946 debut of *Philco Radio Time*, starring Bing Crosby with Bob Hope at his first guest, was recorded on a large wax transcription disc. The following year the show would introduce taped broadcasting to prime time network radio played coast-to-coast.

As a background to the story, it was Nazi Germany who, during World War II, developed tape recording, which had been used to broadcast music and propaganda all day and night. After the war, several German tape recorders were recovered and brought to the U.S.

Guitarist and friend of Bing, Les Paul, brought attention to a technician named Colonel Ranger who assembled one of the recorders and demonstrated it to Bing. He could only produce one a year, according to Les, so it was pointless to expect much. However, John Mullin, another of the technicians, rebuilt the recorders and demonstrated their uses to Bing, who was elated. Mullin tape recorded Bing's first new season Philco show on October 1, 1947. Philco Radio Time became the first recorded and edited show on magnetic tape. Bing was impressed and directed Everett, through Crosby Enterprises, to finance the development of an American version of the German machine to be produced with the Ampex Company.

According to Les Paul, who appeared on that radio show with Bing: "Bing wrote out a check for $50,000.00 and handed it to the Ampex Company, saying, "I don't want an interest in your company, just deliver me 50 machines." Bing eventually sold out his interest in audio tape to the Minnesota Mining and Manufacturing Company.

LES PAUL: "So that's how recording tape machines got to America. Bing and I were a big part of it. It just floated up on our shores and Ampex made a fortune from it."

The Pirates

BING: "I invested a bundle of what the financial lads call 'venture money' into the Pittsburgh Pirates baseball franchise. It's my fervent hope that the Pittsburgh fans will be rewarded for their long-suffering patience with a team of which they can be proud. In a careless moment I promised my four baseball-maniac sons that if Pittsburgh ever got into the World Series, I'd charter a private car and transport them and any number of their buddies eastward for the big event."

For the record: Bing had invested in the Pittsburgh Pirates and Bob Hope had invested in the Cleveland Indians.

Once, Groucho Marx and Bing Crosby found time when they were together in New York City to attend a Dodgers vs. Pirates game at Brooklyn's Ebbetts Field. They hailed a cab in

....
Bing & three
of his boys,
1948
....

New York City, afraid the cabby would not be interested because he would have no fare on the way back:

CABBY: "Where to?"

GROUCHO: (to disguise the real blow) "Chicago!"

CABBY: "Chicago?"

GROUCHO: "You heard me, but just to show you we're nice people, we'll go to Ebbets Field instead."

CABBY: (groaning) "I'd rather drive to Chicago."

GROUCHO: "That's impossible, Pittsburgh isn't playing there."

CABBY: "Say, you look like one of the Marx Brothers."

GROUCHO: "So do you."

Bing owned 20% of the Pittsburgh Pirates Baseball Franchise. Groucho Marx appeared in one Crosby film, *Mr. Music*, in 1950, starring Bing, Peggy Lee and a singing group named the Merry Macs. Groucho sang "Life is So Peculiar."

The Pirate's Den

Besides investments in horse races, oil wells and baseball, Bing once invested in a nightclub. In 1941 Bing and some fellow entertainers, Fred MacMurray, Johnny Weissmuller, Errol Flynn, and Bob Hope, invested in a night club named "The Pirate's Den." At the time the actor Errol Flynn was making a movie about pirates with Warner Brothers. Singer Rudy Vallee thought about the idea and, not wanting to be a lone investor, invited other important celebrities to join with him in the venture.

VALLEE: "Each investor gave one-thousand dollars. The Den was on LaBrea near Beverly and our opening night was covered by Time Magazine and Life Magazine. Opening night worked out, and we had excellent food."

The clanging of bells could be heard upon entering the club. Female patrons were *abducted* by bands of *swashbucklers* and thrown into the brig on some silly charge. Escape was won by screaming until the *brigands* shouted to turn them loose. Each abducted *wench* was awarded a *scream diploma* and was served one of six mystifying drinks. Pirates would act out endless antics and battles. Waiters were lashed and bodies were disposed of in a wheelbarrow. All in all, it was lots of fun, but it didn't last too long.

VALLEE: "It became a lone crusade on my part to keep it all going."

Vallee had lost much money in east coast nightclubs in the past and was afraid to be the only investor. This time his losses were spread out to the disappointment of Bing and his fellow performers.

Over his life Bing had invested in banks, music publishing, an ice cream distributorship, and cattle in South America and the United States. Most of these investments fared poorly. Del Mar, Minute Maid and the oil leases with Bob Hope did pretty well. In 1950 Bob Hope and Bing received 3.5 million dollars each for a successful oil well strike in North Snyder, Scurry County, West Texas. In 1957, Bing stretched his investments in Major League Baseball by buying 5.5% interest in the Detroit Tigers, and in several radio stations in Long Beach, California and Portland, Oregon, as well as an interest in co-ownership of Binglin Stables, a small interest in the Los Angeles Rams football team, and the Crosby Research Foundation, which was

.... 1953 ice cream carton ....

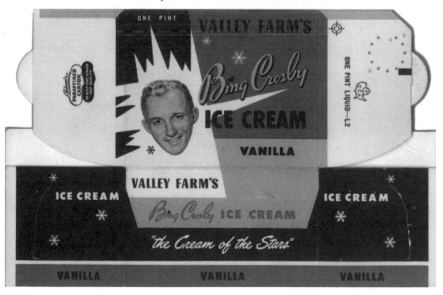

established during the war to encourage the development of products vital to the war effort, namely: a burn remedy called Hydrosulphosol used in Korea during the Korean War; the Shavex, a solenoid which converted electric razors from AC to DC current; transparent plastic raincoats; a pocket lighter; a fire exit lock that precluded fire disasters; and a nylon dip which made it possible to wash nylon stockings and woolens in cold water, just among dozens of other products. All of this was managed by Bing's Attorney, John O'Melveny, in whom Bing had complete confidence over many, many years. He was also appointed guardian of the four Crosby boys' finances by Bing in order to protect their interests.

And, disappointed at his sons' lack of interest in taking over the Elko, Nevada ranch, Bing regrettably disposed of it for one million dollars.

An Insightful 1943 Interview with Bing

Q: How do you fight your tendency towards overweight?

A: By eating a very light dinner, usually only a bowl of soup or a glass of milk.

Q: Are you a sucker for a hard luck story?

A: Yes, but I'm learning.

Q: How many winning horses have you actually had?

A: I'd say my nags have won at least sixty races — and Bob Hope can find 'em in the records.

Q: Whom do you wish you resembled on the screen?

A: In appearance, any reasonably popular star except Hope. In ability, Spencer Tracy.

Q: Have you ever yearned to be taller?

A: Sure! Particularly when I'm with a tall leading lady. I'm five nine, but I could do with six feet very nicely.

Q: Do you sing in the shower?

A: Oh, yes! But good. And the special tile gives me terrific acoustics, I might add.

Q: Are you strict with your children?

A: The only time I really crack down is when they tell a lie, deliberately break up property, or get fresh. I can't stand fresh kids.

Q: What is your pet name for Dixie?

A: I don't have one, although some people call her Dix, which she hates. When I want to rib her I call her by her real name of Wilma.

Q: Do you ever help around the house?

A: Sure, why not? I'm great at making breakfast, especially French toast, and I do a mean job of raking up leaves and carrying off debris and trash. Anything mechanical, however, stymies me; I can't even fix a safety pin.

Q: What is your favorite midnight snack?

A: Anything and everything I can find in the ice box — if Dixie doesn't catch me!

Q: Do you and Dixie have a long-standing argument?

A: Yes, about disciplining the kids. She says I'm too easy on 'em. I don't lick 'em as often as she, but I do a better job of it when a spanking is indicated. Or so I maintain.

Q: What is the least and the most you have been paid for singing?

A: I've worked all night for three bucks and played the drums too, when the band was playing college proms at the University of Gonzaga. On the other hand, one song brought me $50,000 not long ago when a gentleman on the Oakland golf course paid that much for a War Bond in exchange for hearing me warble.

Q: Do you like being a celebrity?

A: Frankly, yes, because I'm a ham.

Q: What do you like least and most about it?

A: The most? The buildup it gives me in the eyes of my kids. After they saw *Road to Morocco*, for instance, I was a big man around the house for a while. Now I'll have to wait until the movie *Dixie* is released before I rate again. Meanwhile Abbott and Costello will be their heroes. The least? Always missing the kick off at football games because autograph hounds tie me up at the stadium gate.

Q: Does it embarrass you to be stared at in public?

A: I'm never aware of anyone staring. Usually they holler at me. It's not embarrassing; I like it.

Q: Do you lose your temper quickly?

A: I don't have any temper to lose. In fact, I can't remember ever getting really mad. I used to wrap a few golf clubs around trees when I missed a shot, but that's not losing your temper and, besides, I don't do it anymore.

Q: What do you find it hardest to forgive?

A: Disloyalty.

PART TWO

Recalled to Life

Kathryn and Bing, the very first interview
(K. Crosby collection)

For the Love of Kathryn

Bing likes Kathryn. Kathryn likes Bing.
BING LOVES KATHRYN. KATHRYN LOVES BING.

"I was never a fan. I never collected Bing Crosby records. I never saw Bing Crosby movies. I fell in love with the man."

Olive Kathryn Grandstaff married Harry L. "Bing" Crosby at St. Anne's, a small Mission style church nestled among a grove of trees in Las Vegas, Nevada, on October 24, 1957, administered by Rt. Rev. John J. Ryan. Leo Lynn, Bing's classmate at Gonzaga, now loyal valet, chauffeur, and movie stand-in, and Kathryn's aunt, Mrs. Guilbert (Mary) Banks, were witnesses.

For Kathryn, it was a day of mixed joy and expectations, perhaps the day of all days. She wore a white suit with a Spanish mantilla on her dark hair. Bing looked neat in a dark pinstripe suit. A simple mass and ceremony were marked by two candles burning brightly on the altar. Her hands clutched her daily missal. When Bing murmured "With this ring I thee wed," Kathryn presented her hand. Bing led the way, taking her elbow, helping her to rise, and motioned when to kneel upon the appropriate moment.

Minutes later they were married. In the church anteroom Bing fought back tears. Kathryn whispered,"It's all right Bing, we'll make it."

*****

"Call me Kathryn. Like my mother, I am Olive Kathryn, but I like to be called Kathryn. As Bing's wife, I'm Mrs. Bing Crosby or Kathryn Crosby, but as an actress I'm Kathryn Grant. Bing belongs to the public. He always has, and that's good. As Kathryn Grant, I've belonged to the public for five years now and I'm very happy about it, but together, we belong to each other and to no one else. Our life as Mr. and Mrs. Bing Crosby will be purely our personal and private affair."

So articulated the young and lovely Kathryn Crosby on April 5, 1958 to magazine writer Pete Martin of the *Saturday Evening Post*.

*****

Olive Kathryn Grandstaff was born on November 25, 1933 in Houston, Texas.

"When I was three, I won my first bathing beauty contest in Robstown, Texas, where my Aunt lived. I was chubby and had bouncy, corkscrew curls like Shirley Temple." At 14, Kathryn won second place in a Texas beauty pageant.

"At fifteen I won the Buccaneer Navy Contest held at Corpus Christi Naval Base near my hometown. We were dressed as pirates. I think I won because I was enjoying the contest and couldn't have cared less if I won."

In Texas there were beauty contests held every week. Kathryn went on to win many such contests, losing only a few along the way.

After high school, Kathryn attended the University of Texas. Her Uncle Leon helped her achieve her initial ingress into the Hollywood scene, where she had hoped to become an actress. Hollywood agent Art Rush, who took an interest in Kathryn, once asked: "Would you be interested in going into movies?" Uncle Leon, who was present, interceded, "Of course, she would!" It was a few years later that her call to Rush became instrumental in Paramount Studios signing Kathryn to a motion picture contract.

"At that time I was working for a Texas newspaper, part of Citizen Newspapers, owned by Glen McCarthy. I got to know two guys at the paper, Bill Sitton and Glen Heath, and later, when I won the Miss Texas contest, I wrote them a long letter. It convinced them to hire me to write a weekly column. I named it *Texas Girl*."

The column was comprised of interesting matters Kathryn was involved with as well as profiles of interesting people she had met. She would describe what a Hollywood movie sound stage looked like, or present readers with a reporter's image of the beautiful beaches in Malibu, something readers in those small, inland Texas towns would find exciting. And she wrote about meeting stars like.....well, Bing Crosby.

"I wasn't a great interviewer. In 1954 I was interviewing Joan Fontaine and Bob Hope on the set of *Casanova's Big Night*.

"I plunged straight into my version of investigative journalism. Bob simply smiled, but his ripely beguiling co-star took umbrage at queries such as, 'How old were you when you made those wonderful films in the thirties, when you won your Oscar in 1941 for your role in *Suspicion*? So how old does that make you now?'

"Joan was perturbed and about to stomp me into oblivion with her four-inch heels when Bob intervened: 'Making allowances for your youth and inexperience, we still can't allow you talk to a great star that way. Now, here's what you should have asked:' "Bob Hope proceeded to set up a series of questions to which Joan *vouchsafed* amused answers that the young reporter hastily noted on her pad. Hope had saved the day with his lesson. Kathryn never forgot that interview. It was the first time she had met the great Hope, and later when she interviewed Hope's long time friend and co-star, Bing Crosby:

"I was ready to snare a superstar and a husband with a far more subtle approach. So, it was Bob Hope, fabulous teacher and later friend, whom I have to thank."

*****

Kathryn's first meeting with Bing Crosby was a breeze. A few months after arriving in Hollywood, she had secured a temporary job in the Wardrobe Department at Paramount Studios. She had tested for film roles at Paramount and was actually under contract, but hadn't begun any work in films up to that point. Upon a delivery of a load of petticoats to *Wardrobe*, she hurried past Rosemary Clooney's dressing room along dressing room row. Bing Crosby was standing in the doorway of his dressing room chatting with Barney Dean, a writer and gag man. Bing had just returned from Europe after filming *Little Boy Lost*.

"Howdy, Tex. What's your rush?"

"No rush, really," returned a surprised Kathryn, coming to a halt.

Two petticoats slipped off her arm. He helped retrieve them.

"Hey, Barney and I are grabbing a little breather while the company moves to another stage. *Y'all* shouldn't hurry so," noted the crooner, teasing about her Texas accent.

Bing welcomed her to his dressing room. Barney offered her a ginger ale. Bing interpreted the photos on the wall, some from the *Road* movies, some from other films.

The conversation drifted to tennis and tea. Bing lit his pipe. After a few minutes she had to go. Bing suggested for her to stop by again for tea and maybe some macaroons.

The second chance meeting found Kathryn guiding visiting Texans on the *White Christmas* set, watching Bing, Rosemary, Danny Kaye, and Vera Ellen do their stuff.

"Hello, Tex!" Again. This time he was peddling a bicycle on the set.

He was charming to the Texans. Then, "Why don't *y'all* drop over after a while?"

Later, on the set he sat next to her and exchanged small talk. Her guests noticed his attention to her, one saying, "He's just very nice, Kathryn. I declare, he has such blue eyes. Did you notice how he looked at you?"

She noticed!

*****

A short time later, and during a break in the filming of *Country Girl*, Kathryn interviewed Bing on the set for her Texas newspaper column.

"Mr. Crosby, because my readers live in ranch country, would you like to tell me a bit about your Elko ranch?"

"With or without drawl?" There was a glint in his eyes, "Is Texas where you were for Christmas?"

"Yes, why?"

"I called your Topanga Canyon number and the man who answered said, 'So you're Bing Crosby; well, I'm Harry Truman,' and hung up on me."

Kathryn laughed. "That was my Uncle Walter."

They finished the interview:

"Why don't you call me Bing and I'll call you Kathryn. Maybe we can continue this interview over dinner — maybe on Sunday? I could pick you up."

"Okay, that will be just fine."

"Bye *y'all*."

She was very young and scared, but thrilled.

*****

Bing suggested a Dubonnet Mist, a rather harmless drink, followed by a heavenly dinner. Bing Crosby was a golfer, a swimmer, and all around sportsman. Kathryn was light on all subjects. Bing was a world traveler. Kathryn had been here and there. Even about art, music and literature, Bing was topping it all. Driving home Bing swung a cappella into "Sometimes I'm Happy," with Kathryn tossing in some harmony; their first duet. On to "You'd Be So Easy to Love," a perfect Crosby song sung to her so sweetly.

The next morning Kathryn tagged herself "Miss Most-Dropped of 1954." To her chagrin Paramount had dropped her, her Texas column was canceled, and, to make things even worse, UCLA dropped her from its Drama Department.

One date followed another, and another. Weeks became months. The months went fast. While Bing was away, they continued their lives through letters. Bing enjoyed writing them, and Kathryn enjoyed receiving them. She didn't know very much about Bing's legendary career, or just how big he really was. Bing always made her feel comfortable, so it didn't matter; in fact, she articulated well before Bing. He liked listening to her opinions and activities. It was music to his ears.

Kathryn found many reasons to love Bing. And Bing surely loved her back. They bantered back and forth about the idea of marrying. Then Bing proposed:

"We were at his Palm Springs home sitting alongside the pool just watching the stars. Our roots had grown strong. We had become really close. Our bond of understanding was valid."

"You mean you might want to marry me?"

"Yes," Kathryn answered, "I believe so."

They set a date. "I was going to be a Spring bride."

They soon became an "item" on the Hollywood scene. They attended the Academy Awards. Bing had been nominated, but lost to Marlon Brando in *"On the Waterfront,"* and didn't seem to mind. Kathryn admired this trait. She also enjoyed the flurry of interest centered on them. There were murmurs:

"There's Bing Crosby."

"Who's she?"

*****

Spring passed. Kathryn and her mother worked on arranging a September wedding. Several dates were set, only to be canceled for one reason or another: Movie making commitments, Bing's insufferable kidney stone problems, Kathryn's schooling, mutual exhaustion, and a surprising change of religious following; (Methodist Kathryn had suddenly wanted to become a Catholic, and it wasn't Bing's idea). She had become affected when she appeared in a USO show in France. In a mass on Christmas Day held in Sacre' Coeur: "The music was beautiful. I needed to be able to worship. I felt at home on that hard wooden kneeler."

So, many sets of plans were scuttled. Or maybe Kathryn wasn't ready for marriage. She went to work and made a series of motion pictures.

On a break in Seattle where Bing took part in ground-breaking ceremonies for the Crosby Library, the press moved in on the couple, inquiring about their forthcoming wedding. Doubts reared again. Was she too young for him? Was he too old for her? Were they each ready? Was the world around them trying to tell them something?

After a talk down at the boathouse, Kathryn decided she would fly home:

"Bing, if I go home now, I won't see you anymore. If we're not supposed to marry, then we're not. We are just drifting. It's not fair. I'll go home content if you will only tell me you don't love me. That's all I ask."

"I love you and I always will."

Kathryn never caught the plane from Spokane. Instead she remained and they tried to work out their problems.

They went to Pebble Beach, California, and while Bing played golf, an interesting thing happened to Kathryn:

"On the beach, a sailor whistled at me, and I smiled. He didn't know me and couldn't have cared less. But, I became aware that I was still free. Something told me I ought to remain that way. That didn't mean I didn't love Bing. But, we were bringing much pain to my family. Things were not in balance. My decision was made: The courtship was finished."

Kathryn went to Los Angeles to pick up her film and television career. She also made a third USO tour to Korea. Upon her return Bing came to her apartment and she served tea, whereupon he invited her to dinner, but she turned him down. Bing didn't seem to understand. She was not happy or sad when he got up to leave: "Thanks for coming by," and they carefully shook hands at the door. A deep void persisted, however.

Kathryn steeped deeper into her work. For her it was a way to a final cure.

A letter from Bing arrived saying he shouldn't have come, and he enclosed her baptismal certificate, now unimportant to her. That had been January. It was now June and nothing from Bing to Kathryn, or Kathryn to Bing.

More time elapsed

With Bing & Kathryn at 1954 Oscar ceremony *(K. Crosby collection)*

while Kathryn flew to Spain to complete filming *The Seventh Voyage of Sinbad*, which gave her much enjoyment for sure while she pretended to be a princess living within the Arabian Nights and slept in a silken bed soaking up the beautiful sounds of Spain. The food, the wine, and learning Castilian Spanish only could have added to her wonderful experience. Kathryn escaped into fantasy, a far cry from the pains of life's decisions and indecisions.

*****

New letters started coming. "I love you. Please let me hear from you."

Invitations, then her rejections. Appeal after appeal. She was tortured. The recent silence was keenly felt by both. Then, a hand delivered letter saying,"Marriage, any time, any place you wish." It was October 22nd.

She tossed and turned, remembering past broken promises and delays. She had to proceed with caution. A call to Aunt Mary, then to proceed to a plan of action. Which way should she go? There was really only one way, she thought.

Aunt Mary: "Kathryn, he sounds so sad." She had been talking with Bing on the phone. "He wants to talk to you and I can't give him your number because I promised I wouldn't."

"I'll be right over."

Kathryn, trembling, arrived at Aunt Mary's. Bing, on the phone, talked with Mary as Kathryn sipped hot tea. What was to be her fate?

Plans were discussed: "We must marry. We need each other. How to get there. Evasive plans to avoid the press. Could I continue my nursing if we married? And what about my acting career? Could I continue that?"

Aunt Mary: "We're taking the five o'clock plane, young lady," she told the gasping, trembling Kathryn.

Bing Crosby and Kathryn Grant were, at last, to become man and wife, to be known forever as Mr. & Mrs. Harry Lillis (Bing) Crosby.

Life with Bing
The New Kids on the Block

"Nobody gave our marriage much of a chance."
Kathryn Crosby.

Kathryn and Bing Crosby would have been married twenty years on October 24, 1977, but only nine days earlier Bing had succumbed on that infamous golf course in Spain after enjoying an18 hole round of golf.

"I'm glad I married an older man. When I married Bing he was already formed, his character was set; in other words, I knew what I was getting. With a younger man you can't tell how he will develop with the years."

Bing took a lot of kidding after the wedding; after all, he was marrying a girl thirty years his junior. Bing's sons took a lot of teasing too, but they were always very nice to Kathryn. The boys became her friends. She did everything possible to insure this for Bing's sake, as well as for her own and the boys themselves. She wasn't their mother and never tried to be. She promoted harmony and respect within the family.

"I've never had my wedding ring off, and I've never asked but I'm sure it's only brass. Bing's manager bought it, and probably didn't want to invest much into something that might not last."

Bing and Kathryn spent a wonderful life together. They shared so much and took pleasure in each other's company. They liked taking walks together, holding hands, and talking about everything and anything. They were best friends. They rarely had guests visit their home. They were simply happy with themselves and would never allow their marriage to become a public affair. Their idea of celebrating a special occasion was to sit at the kitchen table late at night by themselves crunching on a breakfast cereal like Kellogg's Corn Flakes.

St. Anne's in Las Vegas, the little church where Bing and Kathryn were married

The union of Kathryn and Bing Crosby produced three children within the first four years of their marriage, Harry Lillis III in 1958, Mary Frances, Bing's first and only girl in 1959, and, lastly, Nathaniel in 1961. These lucky kids learned a lot from their all-knowing father, while nurtured along by a most-loving mother.

"Bing was a somewhat strict parent, but strict with love — there's a difference. Bing detested sloppiness, could not abide arrogance or profanity and naturally expected good manners from his children. Our children always adored their father — but they also respected him."

In a 1974 interview with Tracy Johnson, Bing talked about his new batch of kids:

"Harry is a serious musical student, studying harmony and composition. He plays the guitar and piano and wants to go to Julliard. He is also very busy in sports, especially tennis. He's not too serious a singer, however, but he sings now and then.

"Mary Frances had trained in ballet for a few years and was studying voice. She has a peculiar quality that you find very seldom in most people. Although quite ordinary and normal, when she gets upon a stage and reads a line or sings, or even dances, something happens. She becomes electrifying and

Kathryn and the kids at the New York World's Fair, 1965 Flushing, NY
(K. Crosby collection)

sparks come forth. I think, for that reason, she has a show business future."

Mary Frances spoke of her father: "In contrast to Mother — who is a soft, warm, affectionate Southern lady — he was a very uncomfortable with expressing his feelings. He'd use sarcasm or criticism to slip in a compliment upside-down. Or we'd hear of his praise from other people. If I kissed him good-night, he'd pull away. If I hugged him too long, he'd squirm. It was fun playing against his resistance, because I knew he secretly loved the tenderness he found so hard to express.

"And growing up as Bing's daughter is something that I am very proud of. I loved being his kid. I am from good stock, as they say. I am proud to have his genes and the genes of my mother in my body. I think they make me strong and talented and good. On a more personal level, it was great because Daddy had always had boys and he never had a girl. He did-n't know what to do with me as a girl. It was terrific. He taught me how to play baseball and how to hunt and fish. I am, to this day, an incorrigible tomboy."

In 1981, that tomboy killed J.R. on *Dallas*, on national television, the act remaining Mary's great claim to TV fame. She will always be remembered for that infamous and das-tardly act. (They say he had it coming.)

Nathaniel is a sports enthusiast. He golfed, played tennis and football, all when he was thirteen. He was taking golf and tennis lessons and was a serious student. Bing had set his eyes on Nathaniel becoming a good athlete.

*****

There was a time at Bing and Kathryn's twenty-five room Holmby Hills home when both families got together for an old fashioned Sunday afternoon in the backyard. Phillip, 25, at the time, and his daughter Dixie Lee, named, of course, after his mother, would play with Dennis' son Duke. Gary, 26, tum-bled with his little sister Mary Frances, while the girls, Dennis' wife Pat, Gary's wife Barbara, Phillip's wife Sandra, and Kathryn discussed — what else — babies. For lunch Kathryn made roast beef, Sandra brought potato salad, Barbara brought a vegetable salad, and Pat contributed a layer cake for dessert. It was parents, babies, brothers, sisters, mothers and fathers enjoying a nice family situation, just like any American family on a summer afternoon. Here, as everywhere, the children, in this case Mary Frances, Duke, Harry, Dennis, Jr., and Dixie Lee, played and the men threw a baseball or football around while their wives discussed recipes and diets.

As in all families, differences existed, but a kindred spirit always brought them together. In this family, Kathryn was the catalyst, a perfect hostess, and always caring with genuine love and interest towards Bing's first children and their families.

Kathryn: "Before our marriage, Bing lived here alone. Now, our families enjoy this great house and every Sunday it becomes alive with the sounds of babies, shop talk and renewed family friendships which bring forth the exciting feelings of restored family life in action."

Traveling with Bing and Kathryn

Bing and Kathryn were both itinerant travelers, almost nomadic in nature. They consistently flew to London, Rome (where they met with the Pope or attended Olympic Games), France, and cities all over the globe. If Kathryn would perform in a play in Chicago, then Bing went to Chicago, usually with one of the kids. Bing would take Kathryn to the Abbey Theatre in Ireland just to see a play, or to Spain just to shoot partridge or view a bullfight. When Kathryn toured with the play *Sabrina Fair*, Bing picked her up in Holyoke, Massachusetts, only to take her to visit Everett Crosby who lived in Salisbury, Connecticut at the time.

They flew to Las Cruces like most people would amber into a town near their neighborhood. They attended dedications or golf outings almost everywhere in the U.S. Bing would ride in a parade as Grand Marshal in Alberta, Canada, or play golf at Mittersill,Austria, on his way to Paris. Trips to Hawaii were frequent. Bing introduced Kathryn to John Wayne on one of their Hawaiian excursions. After a visit to Monaco with Princess Grace, Kathryn flew home and Bing whisked off to Paris. Bing would fly to Ireland alone to see his horse run and win in the Irish Sweepstakes. The travels alone of the new Crosby family could fill a book of its own.

La Casa Crosby at Las Cruces

Casa Crosby, a twelve-room, white stucco, rambling adobe mansion with a red-tiled roof, outfitted in Spanish

Colonial, was constructed in Baja Sur, Mexico, on a hill in 1960 under Bing's supervision. The property overlooked the beautiful *Sea of Cortez* and was completely surrounded by spectacular countryside. It was the relaxing hacienda where Bing and Kathryn chose to spend their needed time off with their three young children.

After the hurricane season ended in March, Bing, Kathryn, Mary Frances, Harry, and Nathaniel gathered up their vacation necessities, climbed aboard a private plane for the four and a half hour flight, checked in with the Mexican authorities in La Paz on the Gulf of California, and completed another ten-minute flight to a private landing strip near the village of Las Cruces, followed, lastly, by a two-mile drive to their *Casa Crosby*.

Baja Sur was discovered by Bing while on a Marlin fishing trip some years before. To Bing it was a perfect place: remote, private, and far from the madding crowd. Kathryn, an outdoor girl who went fishing and hunting with her dad, equally enjoyed the same adventures Bing had always savored.

Finally, arriving at *Casa Crosby*, Bing and Kathryn unloaded the plane and prepared to settle down in the handsome hacienda. The furnishings were collected by Kathryn from stores in La Paz and Mexico City. On Sunday, the family attended the *Little Church*, a colonial missionary style dwelling that was built in the 1930s by the son of a Mexican President. After church, seasoned by years of walking golf courses, Bing and his family would take a long stroll over the locality. Taking precious time to enjoy the family outing at Las Cruces, Bing, Kathryn and the children enjoyed the beach, swimming, fishing, and the ambiance supplied by a beautiful weather under a brilliant Mexican sun. There were spectacular views to savor from the mansion on a hill overlooking a pristine beach drawing gentle waves.

Blood and Sand at Las Cruces

An almost tragic event happened one day in Baja when young Harry was riding with Bing, Kathryn, and Rosemary Clooney, in their little Renault beach wagon. Mary Frances was sitting on Bing's lap and Harry was sitting in the wickerseat.

Bing with munchkins
(K. Crosby collection)

KATHRYN: "There were no windows or doors on this vehicle. The sandy road was a series of deep ruts and bumps. Bing turned a corner to the left just as three year old Harry stood up then suddenly tumbled over the side of the car. I felt an ominous bump as Bing jammed on the brake. He leaped out, dumping Mary Frances into the sand, and raced for Harry. I scrambled out onto the sand and fell almost on top of a small crumpled heap which, thanks be to God, was shrieking its lungs out, my first indication that we hadn't run over Harry's head."

With blood and sand over his face and into his eyes, Kathryn was horrified. Later she realized that one arm was badly bruised and covered with tire marks. She picked up Harry and jumped back into the car. Back at the house she bathed the eye and arranged to fly to a hospital in La Paz. Arriving, she found the old clinic was closed and the new one hadn't yet opened, but they located a doctor, raced back to the old clinic and checked out Harry, finding an eyeball had been scratched. Some of the dirt and sand was too embedded to safely remove, but the doctor assured Kathryn it would all grow out in time on its own. An X-ray proved there was no skull fracture or concussion. They remained at the clinic overnight. At midnight a plane arrived, but it was too dark to fly out of the antiquated airport that had no lights. In the morning Kathryn, Rosemary, and Harry flew to Los Angeles. The pediatrician met the plane and they all drove to Children's Hospital where little Harry safely recovered.

Back in California

In 1965 Bing and Kathryn moved their little family into a French-style mansion at 1200 Jackling Drive in Hillsborough, California. The brick house was built in 1929 on a twelve acre site that included hot houses and a large barn. The great racehorse Seabiscuit had been buried on the property long before Bing had purchased it. Interestingly,Bing's own horse once ran against Seabiscuit and lost. The kids attended local schools where Kathryn sometimes worked as a substitute teacher. Before actually moving in, Bing and Kathryn purchased some antiques from the Hearst warehouse in San Francisco, including some antique paneling material and a large 17th century staircase, replacing the then existing one. It was John Scott

The Crosby Estate

Trotter who perused the Hearst warehouse with Kathryn to choose those and other items.

Today, Hillsborough is a showplace where public tours are conducted and the proceeds go to the Coyote Point Museum. It's the first time the French-style chateau has been open to the public since Bing's passing. The house consists of 32 rooms, a porch, a terrace, a loggia and a kitchen garden. When Bing and Kathryn moved in he had the pool filled with soil, fearing for the safety of the kids, then ages 4 through 7. He also added formal gardens. Much Crosby memorabilia and house artifacts are present throughout the house, including Bing's Oscar. At Christmas, tourists are serenaded by Bing's Christmas recordings. Upstairs is Bing's study, an impressive room with carved wooden walls that were brought there from a 15th century Spanish Castle. In the dining room during the holiday season, the table settings with place cards for Rosemary Clooney, Phil Harris, and other celebrity friends remain there to be seen among Kathryn's silver tea service. In the butler's pantry, visitors can view the Christmas ornaments used in the film *White Christmas*. On the upper level, the delightful rooms of the Crosby children are adorned in a Peter Pan theme. The four bunk beds of the little ones are family originals. Finally, the holly-decked lights and candle holders in the kitchen emphasize the room's original oversized cast-iron woodstove flanked by firewood bundles, and baskets of apples on the window sills. The beautiful *High Society* piano is still in the living room.

*****

Kathryn confessed that she gave Bing some painful moments in their twenty year relationship, like the time she volunteered him to be a master-of-ceremonies for a fund-raiser. Bing would always perform for charity, raising millions of dollars over the years, but was very unhappy about Kathryn committing him without his permission, something he would never have done to her, so he simply didn't show up. He dug in his heels and refused to go, even though it hurt.

"Still, in all our years we never have had a fight, even though we had some sticky moments here and there. Of course, we didn't always see eye to eye. Bing was no-nonsense and disciplined, so disciplined that he can eat one half of a biscuit. He was always witty, tender, and fun-loving; it was impossible to be sad around him."

The sound of Bing Crosby had been woven into the tapestry of many lives. There were never scandals about them. Hollywood tabloids searched for reasons to exploit their marriage, but they were never part of the Hollywood social scene, and never tossed fancy parties like most celebrities of the time. Their marriage was based on a commitment to the welfare of the children, respect for one another, the same reverence for items of importance, and a celebration of the Catholic religion they shared.

Bing Crosby felt very private about life, marriage and death.

KATHRYN: "Bing has said all the lovely words to the very lovely ladies on the big screen, but he had very good writers! Innately, he's very sensitive and I think when it came to saying words that would commit him, he would be double reticent without his script. He wrote letters like weather reports."

Kathryn on Television

BING: "Kathryn had her own show on television. She did it five times a week at nine a.m. She interviewed authors in town who wanted to promote a book, or actors about their latest film or show. She's had a lot of doctors on with theories about education, or about medicine, operations, inoculations and a wide, wide field of all subjects. In fact, my pal Phil Harris once

appeared talking about one of his favorites, Southern cooking, and things like that. She taped the show in advance and enjoyed doing it. The show included people like actress Jean Simmons, funny gal Hermoine Gingold, the writer Garson Kanin and whoever had been in town and was interesting."

*****

In November 1975, Bing and Kathryn had been interviewed in their Hillsborough home by television host Mike Douglas, and it became a unique delight and rare event for viewers of Douglas' Christmas season show. Bing closed out the interview when he casually strolled around the house singing "That's What Life Is All About," while taking short swings with a golf club.

On March 3, 1977, at the Ambassador Auditorium in Pasadena, California, Bing fell off a stage deep into a lower elevator-stage after taping a 90 minute television special celebrating his 50 years in show business. It was a serious fall. There were no broken bones, but complications persisted. The extent of the injuries he suffered were unknown at that moment, although a ruptured disc in his lower back soon became apparent. He was unable to stand or walk, and the pain was difficult to endure. Luckily, Bing had grabbed onto a piece of scenery that broke his fall, or God knows if he would have survived it at all.

KATHRYN: "Do you know what Bing did when he was taken out on the stretcher to the ambulance? Trying to keep things normal he sang 'Off we go into the wild blue yonder...' Can you imagine? Through it all, I was happy that he was alive."

Over later years Bing frequently fell victim to kidney stone problems and was hospitalized a number of times.

"Although we did not know what was in store for us in the fall of 1977, Bing and I had an otherwise wonderful year. In London, we took walks together around Piccadilly Circus. From London we went on to Scotland where Mary Frances and I performed *The Heiress* on stage in Edinburgh. Bing, Harry, and Nathaniel traveled all over England, Scotland and Germany. And Bing took us all on a quick trip to Paris, but he was smart enough to do it on Saint's Day, when all the stores were closed and we couldn't buy anything."

In "My Life with Bing," Kathryn presented her total life with Bing in story with a great collection of photographs.

"Since Bing's passing in Spain, I've been very much involved in an appraisal of our life together. I am sustained in my loss by the love, the prayers, the strength and the affection of our children and of the people all over the world who have loved Bing.

"Near the end Bing had to conserve strength, and he did so with great discipline. I don't know many people who get a standing ovation for just walking on stage, but Bing did every night. The audiences were magnificent. They treasured every moment that he sang. On the night of the final performance, there we were all on stage. Rosey Clooney kissed me and then we all kissed everyone on stage, including pianist Joe Bushkin who led the quartet, and Ted Rogers, a comedian. We were all hugging and kissing as Bing was speaking and we all kidded him too. We had never done that before. And we don't know exactly know why we did it then. But we will always be glad that we did. It was almost as if we were doing it for everyone, an expression of affection from and to Bing."

For Kathryn and us all, Bing's legacy will be always present.

"His music lives, his films live, the gentle humor that he displayed is a touching, living wondrous thing. His eyes will never dim and his beauty will never diminish."

Kathryn's Personal Press Report

Kathryn Crosby is a cultural ambassador to the world. From the Music Box Theater on Broadway to the Red Torch Theater in Siberia, Russia, Kathryn lights up any theater marquee with her brilliant stage craft, her warm and effusive personality, and her delightful sense of humor. By her good works on stage and off, Kathryn transcends all geographical and political boundaries.

After a year on Broadway playing Melissa in Rodgers and Hammerstein's *State Fair*, Kathryn traveled to the Red Torch Theater in Siberia to star in the Russian premier of *Hello, Dolly*, her second tour-de-force in Russia. Now a favorite, she returned in 1998 to star in *The Lion in Winter*.

Kathryn's many stage roles include *Margaret in Dear Brutis; Hero in Much Ado About Nothing; Cordella in Sabrina; Doris in Same Time Next Year; and Sarah in Guys and Dolls.* She also starred in national productions of Peter Pan, Mary, Mary, The Prime of Miss Brodie, I Do, I Do, Arms and the Man, The Guardsman, and Oh! Coward.

Of course, Kathryn is an accomplished author, a Registered Nurse, and is fluent in German, French, Spanish and Russian.

Kathryn has hosted the fourth Reinhard Foodservice Pro-Am Golf Tournament as a demonstration of her dedication to the support of young aspiring actors Beyond Broadway.

Much of Kathryn's current travels involve a timeless effort of concentrated activity to advance the legacy of her husband. She is revered by Bing fans everywhere.

Today, Harry Lillis III lives in New York City and is involved in the stock market. He appeared in television interviews after the events of September 11, 2001, having been an actual witness to the attack when he was on his way to work at Merrill-Lynch near the World Trade Towers. Nathaniel is in the business of golf and lives in Scottsboro, Arizona. Mary Frances, who has dropped the Frances, is enjoying being a new mom to little Benjamin Brodka at her home in Malibu, California, while doting grandmother Kathryn enjoys talking much about her "little Angel." Mary is also the owner of the Las Cruces property, a gift from her parents.

Losing Bing

BING: "I love golf. If I ever die I want it to be on a golf course."

FRANK SINATRA: "Bing leaves a gaping hole in our music and in the lives of everybody who loved him, and that's just about everybody."

October 14, 1977

While playing golf in Spain just outside of Madrid, Bing Crosby collapsed and passed away while walking to the locker room at the La Moraleja Golf Club after completing an 18 hole round of golf. He and a Spanish champion had defeated two other Spanish champions by only one stroke. He and the others, Manuel Pinera, Valentin Barrios and Cesar de Zulueta were walking side by side, talking. Bing was matched with Pinero and Barrios had been matched with de Zulueta.

"Bing had a seizure and fell," Barrios reported. "We thought he had just slipped and fell. He injured his head slightly. We took him into the clubhouse and administered oxygen and cardiac tonic injections, but nothing would help. It was no use. It was too late."

Bing was seventy-four.

There was a delayed reaction to the news. The world remained in denial for a while. Then, the usual press inquires to those he knew began in earnest. Friends, business associates, fellow actors and singers were pestered for statements and reminisces.

Early on the morning of Tuesday, October 18, 1977, final services were held for Bing Crosby at St. Paul's Catholic

Kathryn and Harry Crosby at Bing's funeral
(K. Crosby collection)

Church in Westwood, a suburb of Los Angeles. Interment followed in nearby Holy Cross Cemetery, Inglewood, in the same plot where his parents and first wife, Dixie Lee, are buried. Present were Rosemary Clooney, Bob and Dolores Hope, Phil Harris and his wife, Alice Faye, and his sons Gary and Harry Lillis III among the pallbearers.

Flush to the ground, Bing's gravestone was set in place as an eternal marker, ironically mis-marked as 1904-1977. To Bing, numbers were not important, but to the world of music, his numbers were the highest.

*****

Poignant message from Bing Crosby in his own words just days before he died.

"I'm certainly pleased to have the use of some of this space because I want to try and level a base canard that has gained some currency lately in the Press, in a book or two, on TV and in radio interviews.

It is alleged by some careless people that I am a loner, a cold fish without sentiment or convivial instincts. Now I don't suppose there are many people who really care or who are really interested in whether I'm any of these things or all of them.

But, I care. A lot.

My description of a loner would be a recluse, an introvert — a man insecure and deeply introspective. Now, I really don't think

I'm a loner. I'm not very demonstrative. I don't gush, wring my hands or beat my bosom. The only thing that can really arouse my ire is to miss a 2-foot putt when it means the match.

I really think I'm extremely gregarious. Actually, I know more people from more different walks of life and levels of society than anyone I

....
Mary and Nathaniel Crosby at Bing's funeral *(K. Crosby collection)*
....

ever heard of except per-
haps only Bob Hope — and,
of course he's ubiquitous.

I have played golf, shot,
fished, and consorted with
kings, princes, heads of
state, jockeys, seniors,
juniors, pros, — both men
and women — doctors,
lawyers, famous amateurs
male and female, artists,
painters, hustlers, drunks,
financiers, touts, writers and
scientists, every kind of athlete in practically every
country in the world, and on
practically every famous golf course that exists.

Bob and
Dolores Hope
at Bing's
funeral

Puzzling over how this negative opinion got around — that
I was a loner — I think I might have come up with some of the
reasons why. Since I first achieved any success or stature, I
have always traveled more or less alone.

When I came to work, I drove down in my car. If I attended a function or a party, or went to a football match or baseball game or boxing or whatever kind of public event, I either
went alone or with members of the family or maybe one or two
other guys. I have never had an entourage or a retinue trailing
along behind me. Something like this would disturb me — to
be always accompanied thus. It attracts attention. I'd worry
about them.

It's only natural, I suppose, when people see me drive up
alone, or walking along enroute to work or whatever, they
must say, He's a loner. But I love to walk. I love to walk alone.
That's when I do some of my best thinking — or practically all
of my thinking. Sentimental? Acutely. When I see three U.S.
athletes mount the risers at the Olympic Games to receive the
medals, and they play our National Anthem, I'm very misty
eyed. Newsreels of TV films of American troops in faraway
places fighting, suffering and dying affect me deeply.

It makes me very sad to see people embarrassed or treated
shabbily in public. Honestly, I would have to say that I'm really a softy. I never had a disagreement with anyone in any cast
of any picture I ever worked in. Truly.

I had great fun and many laughs with most of them. I can't think of a single film in which we didn't have laughs, gags, ribs going all the time. A lot of people have a mental image of me as a guy who never really worked hard at anything in his life. I'd like to correct that little illusion. I think I've worked hard at a lot of things, but because I liked doing them I guess they came off as easy, and it looked as though I was just waltzing through them without a thought in the world.

Doesn't John Wayne do pretty much the same thing? And look how the Durable Duke is still going strong after some 46 years. One ray of hope that I see on the horizon is the increasing interest in nostalgia, both on the screen and the Broadway stage.

There was a lot of wonderful creativity in many of the old days — note that I didn't say "good old days" — even in the Depression era of the 1930s. There are always better days ahead, if we just make the most of them — and that's a thought I'd like to leave with the new generation. I love show business. Every facet of it. And I'm extremely grateful for what it has done for me. I would be nothing without it.

But, I'm worried now. Pornographic pictures, dirty books and magazines seem to be beyond any kind of control. I was laid up for five or six weeks lately — hospitalized — and, of course, I saw lots and lots of TV. It became apparent to me that very slowly and very subtly writers and producers are working in nudity, permissiveness, irresponsibility, profanity, scenes of semi explicit sex, provocative dialogue, smutty innuendoes and situations into their shows. Moral responsibility is almost indiscernible.

Now I abhor censorship. Another word I dislike is boycott. But the inability of the former to be useful will surely produce the latter. Already there are little groups all over the country — groups of concerned people who want to so something about this before it's too late. Let me tell you something. If they all get together and they become a nationwide organization of fifteen or sixteen million people and they tell some of the big advertisers that they will stop buying their products unless they clean up their shows — impact? You bet. Now I don't condone boycott any more than I do censorship, but it could happen.

It's my fervent prayer that responsible people in the business — people of principle — will exert their influences in an effort to eliminate this highly objectionable material."

Bing's last Christmas Special on television was broadcast on CBS on November 30th, 1977. Bing and David Bowie performed duets of two great Christmas songs, "Peace on Earth" and "Little Drummer Boy."

Commemorations

The Gonzaga Library:

Gonzaga University's Crosby Library was opened on November 3, 1957, a gift to the University from its most famous alumnus, Harry L. "Bing" Crosby, Class of 1924. Recognized nationally at the time of its dedication as a superlative expression of library design, the building is on three levels and of modular construction. Its facade of red Minnesota granite faces Boone Avenue. Crosby Library, the intellectual heart of the university, is appropriately located astride the exact geometric center of the Gonzaga Campus.

Aside from the comprehensive collections, there is a Crosbyana Room, which is of special interest to most visitors. It contains the personal memorabilia of Bing's career. His many gold records and his Oscar for the film *Going My Way* are quite popular. It also includes personal papers, awards, scripts, scores, and other displays.

Bing's association with the library grew from his long

Crosby Bronze Statue and Gonzaga Student Center

friendship with classmate Rev. Francis Corkery, S.J., who served as President of Gonzaga University from 1945 to 1957. In 1957 Bing organized a television special to secure the remaining funds for construction of the library. The telecast was held on CBS on October 13, 1957, and was sponsored by Ford Motor Company to, ironically, introduce their new Car of the Future, the Edsel. Featured were Louis Armstrong, Frank Sinatra, Rosemary Clooney, and Bob Hope. A blockbuster cast and show, it later won an Emmy as the best variety special of that year.

At the commemoration of the library, Bing and Kathryn attended and received the collegiate kudos of the Jesuit officials, alumni, and students alike with surprise. "Say, how about that," Bing muttered to Kathryn. With a Doctorate of Music draped around his neck, Bing stood up, looked at his oversized flowing black robe, and addressed the huge outdoor crowd: "I wish Hope could see me now."

In March, 1979, England honored Bing by installing a unique bronze plaque of his countenance that measured about two feet square, showing Bing with a pipe perched between his teeth. It hung in the lobby of the London Palladium. The dedication and presentation were made by his friend Bob Hope.

Bing was inducted into the Radio Hall of Fame in Chicago on October 11, 1998. Personally appearing there, Kathryn graciously accepted the coveted award for her husband. Others who attended were Bob Hope, Groucho Marx, Arthur Godfrey, Jack Benny, and Fred Allen.

....
Bob Hope and
Sir Lew Grade
*(R. Grudens
collection)*
....

PART THREE
People and Things

Bing and Bud Freeman jam at Eddie Condor's Jazz
Club in Greenwich Willage, NY
(R. Grudens collection)

The Crosby Musical Links and Early Influences:
Bill Challis, Bix Beiderbecke, Frank Trumbauer,
Eddie Lang, Wingy Manone, Joe Venuti, Jack Teagarden

Bill Challis

Meeting Bill Challis — Architect of the Swing Era

A traveling salesman peddling building materials to lumber and masons material yards in the late 1960s, I first met Bill Challis, a tall and then portly, although dignified, suit and tie-dressed clerk at Plander's Cement Block Yard in Uniondale on Long Island. He just didn't seem to fit in this dingy and very dusty concrete block manufacturing plant in nearby Uniondale: a definite fish out of water. I was compelled to inquire why he worked behind the counter of this hopelessly dirty office, fastidiously writing up neatly penned routing tickets for trucks that delivered building blocks to construction sites, when he appeared to be, and acted more like an executive who got lost on his way to a Wall Street CEO's office. Then, he revealed his amazing story to me.

*****

An arranger named Bill Challis, who once worked in Jean Goldkette's band as a saxophone player and arranger in the mid-twenties, was way ahead of his time harmonically and rhythmically. Fortunately he became a true Crosby link. Challis, the renowned jazz arranger, earned his stellar reputation through innovative arrangements written earlier for the bandleader pioneer, Goldkette. Later, he wrote scores for jazz great "King of Jazz" orchestra leader Paul Whiteman, famed cornetist Leon "Bix" Biederbecke, Tommy and Jimmy Dorsey, and a young vocalist named Bing Crosby, lead singer of the Whiteman Band as one of the Rhythm Boys. In his autobiography "Call Me Lucky" Bing described Challis: "Bill Challis is a progressive arranger who cooked up vocal licks for recordings and for the stage. Where would we all be without arrangers like Bill Challis? How lucky I was to be a part of that great era?"

Bing, Bill Challis, Frankie Trumbauer, and "Bix" Biederbecke kept close company when they all worked for Paul Whiteman. Bill spent time working with Bing, suggesting techniques to improve Bing's phrasing and mannerisms. Bing was always eager to absorb ideas from his counterparts, which he would always put to work hopefully to improve himself musically and vocally. Challis helped him the most. His bright and bouncy arrangements inspired the impressionable Crosby. Bing could sing well and filled any stage with his personable, casual presence, but there was a lot to learn, and Challis was the great instructor in those fledgling days. Challis taught and Bing eagerly learned. Challis realized that Bing was an emerging, sensational musical talent. His arrangements, geared to Bing's voice quality and delivery, were always on the mark, and nicely moved Bing's repertoire forward. It wouldn't be long before Bing would muster up the courage to journey out to thrive as a single act and become America's most beloved and popular singer of all time. As Bing has acknowledged, Bill Challis was the catalyst.

Challis' pioneer jazz arrangements of "Dardenella" and "I'm Comin' Virginia" (including Bing's vocal) were influential to the advancement of jazz. By the late sixties, however, Bill Challis' career was at an obvious standstill.

"After the Big Band Era sort of ended, most of the guys moved on to Hollywood to play and arrange for film studios. Sure, it's good money, all right, but I didn't like California," he said while we sipped some tea in his backyard located on an inlet in the Village of Massapequa on Long Island's south shore in 1965. "My home here keeps me happy, so I remained behind. There is no work for me in New York these days so I took this job at Plander's in Uniondale. I also have my garden that I love."

Bill and his brother Evan eventually moved back to their boyhood home in Harvey's Lake, near Wilkes-Barre, Pennsylvania, where they permanently retired.

The full story of Bill Challis and his contributions to jazz and popular music are well documented in a chapter called "Bix and Bill" in Gene Lee's excellent book, "Waiting for Dizzy."

Eddie Lang — First Jazz Guitarist

Another important Crosby link, jazz guitarist Eddie Lang (nee Salvatore Massaro) certainly influenced the young singer. Lang moved Bing along musically as they performed on their

Top: Bing and Eddie Lang, 1932 *(R. Grudens collection)* Bottom: Bing and Joe Venuti on Radio CBS

innovative, popular recordings. Lang has accompanied a line-up of music greats: Ruth Etting, Bessie Smith, the Boswell Sisters, Louis Armstrong, and Al Jolson.

Bing felt very comfortable with Eddie Lang, always insisting he be included as his accompanist during radio and theatrical shows, in recording sessions, and in films. It was a genuine partnership: Bing's voice and Eddie's guitar, Eddie usually perched on a stool close to Bing, both sharing a single microphone. Eddie clearly guided Bing's phrasing. His noted arpeggios (the playing of the tones of a chord in rapid succession rather than simultaneously), performed in just the right places for Crosby, paced him along perfectly. The Crosby-Lang recording of "Please" with Anson Week's orchestra is a shining example, as is "I Kiss Your Hand Madam." Bing is typically, comfortably nasal on both, very satisfying recordings.

Before Eddie Lang, the guitar was a chordal rhythm instrument, but Lang, with his incredible rhythmic drive, became a significant soloist. His single string concept was borne in the blues tradition, elevating him to pioneer status, to be followed by those who became enamored of his style. This authentic style kept him in demand for dances and recording sessions. He regularly performed on recording sessions with jazz violinist Joe Venuti.

BING: "Eddie possessed a tremendous ear and had a stroke on the guitar that nobody had employed up until that time. It was a marvelous accompaniment to sing a rhythm song to. It just made you feel like you wanted to ride and go."

Bing and Eddie became close personal friends. Unfortunately, a fatal event befell Lang. Immediately after an elective tonsillectomy (decided upon due to chronic pain Lang experienced with laryngitis) and the immediate subsequent development of a post operative embolism and unnoticed hemorrhaging by an attending nurse, Lang lost his life at twenty-nine. Bing was completely devastated. For him, no one could ever replace Lang. The two had worked as one. It had been a musical team growing day-by-day, and the two found matching talents that catapulted them to great celebrity. Bing Crosby financially supported Kitty Lang for the remainder of her life in accordance with a promise he had made to his playing partner and dear friend, Eddie Lang.

Bix Beiderbecke and Frankie Trumbauer

"Bix" Beiderbecke and Frankie Trumbauer were members of the famous Jean Goldkette Orchestra of the 1920s. So were Tommy and Jimmy Dorsey, Joe Venuti, Russ Morgan, Bill Challis, Artie Shaw, and Glenn Miller. Sometimes Trumbauer would lead the band, as it was Goldkette's habit to select certain players to lead now and then. Goldkette didn't like being a front man, just owner and manager. Trumbauer brought Bix into the band at a time when he was leading it in New York. While a member of Paul Whiteman's Orchestra, "Bix" Beiderbecke, like Lang, passed away at a very young age.

BING: "It wasn't booze that killed "Bix". He wasn't an alcoholic. He was a jolly absentminded sort of fellow, but he was so totally immersed in music that he never ate or slept properly. His health broke from exhaustion. Of course, it seemed none of us went to bed in those days. It's amazing that some of us survived."

This genius of jazz, legendary cornet player Leon "Bix" Beiderbecke broke much musical ground in his very short life.

Another fellow-member of Paul Whiteman's famed King of Jazz orchestra, Frankie Trumbauer, friend of Crosby, "Bix" Beiderbecke and Jack Teagarden, became the Crosby style — laid back-musician, a champion of the saxophone. Nicknamed *Tram*, he was one of the great sax players of the era. When he, Crosby, Biederbecke, and Bill Challis would practice singing and playing around the piano in a speakeasy, they would work out musical concepts and suggest vocalizing strategies to Bing, which, as stated earlier, he absorbed, then subsequently utilized.

Bing always credited Eddie, Tram, "Bix" and Bill Challis as his musical teachers. Bing genuinely enjoyed what Beiderbecke and Trumbauer would dish up. Challis would provide the lead sheet and invoke his own jazzy ideas into the session.

One of Bing's best with Whiteman was Bill Challis' arrangement of "You Took Advantage of Me," with "Bix" Biederbecke on cornet and Frankie "Tram" Trumbauer on alto sax playing alternate phrases, and highlighted by Bing's unforgettable chase chorus.

It is safe to say Bing Crosby's association with these great musicians unequivocally affected his singing style and changed him in midstream by developing styles for him to

Bix'n'Bing
with the Paul Whiteman Orchestra
a twenty track album of their finest moments

ASV

follow. On one of Bing's early recordings, "'Taint So," Trumbauer performs an accompanying solo on a bassoon, of all instruments, a neat backup to a very interesting and well arranged recording. In 1932, when Bing was in Chicago, he recorded "With Summer Coming On," "Love Me Tonight," "Cabin In the Cotton" and "Some of These Days" with Trumbauer's Orchestra.

Bix and Bing

Joseph Matthew "Wingy" Manone

Wingy Manone, a one-armed trumpet player who once led his own band, appeared with Bing Crosby in one memorable film, *Rhythm on the River*. In the film, he played his trumpet in a spontaneously spirited sequence where Bing and other musicians literally marched around a circle inside a pawn shop performing the title song "Rhythm on the River," a worthy Crosby-Manone musical rendition if ever there was one. A regular guest on Bing's radio programs, Wingy Manone was a very personal friend to Bing. He had lost his arm in a streetcar accident when he was a child.

"Wingy was another member of the jazz cult, as we called it, whose talents we used in some of my pictures. He worked for us in *Rhythm on the River*, made in 1940, one of my favorite films. Everyone knows Wingy had one arm, that's why we called him *Wingy*. Jazz violinist Joe Venuti, another member of the clan, used to send Wingy one cuff link for Christmas."

RHYTHM ON THE RIVER
Johnny Burke and James Monaco

When you hear a real hep-cat,
Take a chorus in A-flat
That's the rhythm of the river
You know what that means,
He comes from New Orleans
When a drummer starts to ride
And a rim shot breaks the hide
That's the rhythm of the river
Can't mistake that beat
He comes from Basin Street
Now, how do you like a Bugle Call Rag?
You played it in waltz for a Dixieland jazz
I'll take the words right out of your mouth
Got to play it the same as down South
In New York or any town
When a band
swings way lowdown
That's the rhythm of the river
Not the Hudson, but
Just Mississippi mud.

When Bing had Wingy play a few numbers in *Rhythm On the River*, Wingy couldn't read the elaborate orchestration. For two and a half hours, Wingy tried to pick it up, and when it was suggested to Bing that maybe Wingy shouldn't play the part, he refused to let him go. Bing worked it out with Wingy by singing the part until he finally got it down pat, with a few tricky riffs tossed in. For Bing, he was the authentic man for the job, a living jazzman.

Bing in *Rhythm on the River*, 1940

Like most of Crosby's cronies, Wingy never learned to read music. It was said that he always wanted to play in a big orchestra. Once, Benny Goodman promised that if Wingy ever learned to read notes he would give him a chance to blow his horn in the brass section of his band. Well, Wingy learned to read and wired Goodman to ask for the train fare to join him. Goodman sent the money and Wingy boarded a train from L.A. to New York and joined the band, as promised.

Bing and Wingy Manone in *Birth of the Blues (Paramount)*

BING: "Wingy took his place in the brass section and at the rehearsal they put the third cornet part in front of Wingy and Benny gave the downbeat. Of course the spots meant nothing to Wingy and he was lost after the opening bar or two. Benny came over to him and said, 'I thought you learned to read,' and Wingy replied, 'I did. But man, it's amazing how rusty you can get on those long, cross country train trips.'"

Wingy Manone would contribute his services when Bing needed him for building popularity for his Del Mar Turf Club. The shows, with artists like Louis Armstrong, Phil Silvers, Bob Hope and others performing would sometimes last until morning. One morning at about five o'clock Wingy was playing "Muskrat Ramble" when a committee of trainers came over from the stables to complain that his horn playing was disturbing the horses. They were shagging and Lindy Hopping around their stalls and losing their rest, just like people. Oh, that Wingy!

Wingy Manone also recorded duets with Kay Starr, (who, of course, later sang with Glenn Miller and created a great career for herself), and was considered a Louis Armstrong imitator. Manone never objected to that label since he considered himself a follower of Armstrong, certainly one of his idols.

Wingy Manone will always be remembered for his New Orleans-style trumpet playing and rhapsodizing into musical nonsense set forth in rasping, spitting, and growling tones, sometimes referred to as Chicago Style playing.

Jack Teagarden — Big T

BING: "Jack Teagarden is the great jazz trombonist, one half of the famous "Big Little Gate" who played with Whiteman when I sang with the band way back when."

Bing would describe his friend Jack Teagarden as "Big Gate" and Jack's brother, Charlie, who played jazz trumpet, as "Little Gate," because he was smaller. To many others Jack was also known as Big T. Teagarden learned to play the trombone without any help whatsoever. Arriving in New York from Texas in 1927 at the age of twenty-two, Jack began his recording career, then advanced on to playing with the great Paul Whiteman Orchestra, where he met Bing.

After Whiteman, Jack formed and led his own band from 1939 to 1947 with a stellar group of musicians and vocalists, finally linking up with the Louis Armstrong All-Stars for four years. He reformed his band once again that continued performing until his passing. Jack Teagarden was an enterprising jazz vocalist. That's where Bing came in as they joined up for the film *The Birth of the Blues* in 1941 that also starred a young Mary Martin, later famous for her original role on Broadway as

Jack Teagarden (R. Grudens collection)

Nellie Forbush in Rodgers and Hammerstein's great musical *South Pacific.* Bing, Mary, and Jack shared vocals on tunes like "Wait Til the Sun Shines, Nellie," and Cole Porter's "The Waiter and the Porter and the Upstairs Maid" which they later recorded with Jack's Orchestra.

BING: "Nice piece of material was 'Nellie.' Joe Lilly arranged it. I always felt that was the reason for its success. A beautiful job of arranging, putting a song together and developing it to a climax."

Jack also backed Bing on the commercial recording of "The Birth of the Blues."

BING: "Jack was cast in the film as one of the members of a band and sat with his legs over the tailgate of a wagon — the way the New Orleans bands once played — while he made with the sliphorn."

JACK: "Those wagons actually toured the streets in the old days. Us tailgate musicians did not play dirges at funerals. We figured the one who was gone would have preferred an upbeat tune as they departed us."

Jack's engaging Southern drawl fell somewhere between Louis Armstrong and Bing Crosby, his regular singing partners. Jack's demeanor and appearance, which was tall and handsome with a squared jaw, and his open face and wide eyes that were kept narrowed, allowed him to enjoy parts in films and a place on the bandstand. Occasionally, some folks mistook him for the fighter Jack Dempsey. Some even thought he was part American Indian, but his parents came from Germany. The unmistakable sound of his voice was a distillation of his sentimental playing delivered in a light baritone combined with a Southern drawl, a kind of lay-me-down to-sleep style, especially when he gathered friends around while singing "I've Got a Right to Sing the Blues."

ARVELL SHAW: (Bassist for 25 years in Armstrong's All-Stars.) "I liked to sing the songs Jack Teagarden played, and I would back him on bass. He sang ' Stars Fell on Alabama,' his signature theme, 'After You've Gone,' and my favorite ' A Hundred Years from Today.' Like Louis, Jack was one of the great musicians."

Joe Venuti — The Fabulous Fiddler

Joe Venuti, another Bing insider like Trumbauer, Beiderbecke, Challis, Lang, and Teagarden, started out in South Philadelphia with Eddie Lang as partners in a lot of duet recordings.

After leaving Jean Goldkette, Venuti formed his own first band in the early thirties with sidemen that added up to a who's who of musicians. Most of the great performers from the

Goldkette, Whiteman, and California Ramblers organizations recorded with him. His very young vocalist was Kay Starr, mentioned earlier, whom he discovered singing at a Memphis, Tennessee radio station.

Venuti, an absolute clown, was associated with endless amounts of humorous incidents that have marked him a legend. He would never tolerate criticism from anyone, including his audience. He once nailed the shoes of one of his musicians to the floor because he tapped his shoe too much during performances.

Irreparable Joe Venuti, 1950s

A "hot" jazz violinist, Venuti developed unorthodox methods of performing. Benny Goodman once said that Venuti and Lang were his two favorite musicians, calling Venuti "...the first fiddle-player to make sense in a jazz band."

Bing christened him the *Fabulous Fiddler*. "Undoubtedly," recalled Bing, "Venuti helped age Whiteman. Paul once gave him a violin solo assignment for a very formal concert. Joe asked Paul in front of the audience to let him use his violin. Shrugging, Paul handed his violin to Joe. Joe played a number, then pretended to get his bow tangled in the strings. Finally, in false exasperation, while the audience went into hysterics of mirth, he chewed up Whiteman's fiddle, crunching it with his strong white teeth and spitting out the pieces." Venuti was one of the world's great practical jokers.

According to Bing, Joe Venuti had only one rule. "If he says he's going to do a thing, you'd better believe him, because it's a certainty, no matter how crazy or goofy it sounds."

There were so many wild stories about Joe Venuti.

BING: "High on my personal list of blinding highlights were the great duets of Joe Venuti and Eddie Lang when they recorded together and when they played a specialty performance."

One of Venuti's 1950s albums was labeled "The Mad Fiddler from Philly." Very appropriate!

Jack Kapp,
Al Jolson
and Bing,
1947
*(courtesy
Decca)*

The Power of Bing's Decca Recordings

*Martin Block-Legendary WNEW, New York Disc Jockey: "I
want to say that if there is any one guy in the world who made
disc jockeys popular, it was a fellow named Bing Crosby."*

Before Decca, Bing recorded over 100 sides with
Brunswick Records from 1931 through 1934 under the supervision of its manager Jack Kapp. Notable were "Just One More
Chance," "Brother, Can You Spare a Dime," and "Dinah" with
the Mills Brothers.

Jack Kapp first recorded Bing Crosby for his newly formed
Decca Records in Los Angeles on August 8, 1934. Bing
remained exclusively with Decca until December 31, 1955.
Bing was a favorite of Jack Kapp and he took special interest
in his recording career. He enjoyed Bing's casualness and ultimate cooperation during recording sessions. He wisely scheduled Bing to record with almost every known artist of the day.

He expanded Bing's repertoire in recording a mixed cornu-copia of blues, country, patriotic, ballads, classics, religious, Hawaiian, cowboy, Irish, and even operatic arias. Bing was skeptical about recording such material, feeling his range was limited.

"Jack Kapp was wise enough to have me work with a vari-ety of bands and sing duets with a variety of different artists, so as to give the listeners a change of pace. This policy helped keep me alive as a recording artist long after the average per-former was washed up."

Kapp's affirmative opinion of Bing Crosby's ability sur-passed his opinion of all other performers on the Decca staff of artists. He knew Bing's talents were a cut above, so he had him work with many arrangers and whenever a respected orches-tra was available, he engaged them to record with Bing. Kapp prevented Bing from becoming type-cast. Bing remained total-ly faithful to Jack Kapp and Decca Records for just over 20 years.

"The idea of working for someone else was preposterous to me, and I never gave any other offers serious consideration. With Jack I felt that I was in the hands of a friend and that whatever he told me to do was right."

A fellow named Joe Perry supervised the Decca dates. "Of all the artists I have worked with in 20 odd years, Bing was the easiest and fastest to make records."

Bing had the approval of all songs he recorded for Decca, and he refused to sing any song he didn't like.

Patty Andrews of the Andrews Sisters felt the same way about Decca Records and its President. Her own career had received identical beneficial treatment, allowing the trio to proliferate with similar results. The Andrews Sisters were Bing's apparent favorite vocalists, and he preferred working with orchestra leader John Scott Trotter, as well. Trotter served as Bing's musical director for many years.

Bing recorded two sides with his wife, Dixie Lee: "A Fine Romance," and the better "The Way You Look Tonight," which nicely showcased Dixie Lee's charming voice. She was shy about singing and would never upstage her husband.

Kapp had Bing record songs from his movies made with Paramount Pictures and other Hollywood studios during those

Decca promotes Bing in 1933
(Intl Crosby)

Decca years, including the tremendous hit that charted for 20 years, "White Christmas." It was recorded by Bing twice: once in 1942 and again in 1947, implementing the exact arrangement. The Guiness Book of Records declared "White Christmas" to be the best-selling recording of all time.

*****

Some of Bing's singing partners, vocalists or musical leaders, were: The Boswell Sisters (only 3 sides), The Andrews Sisters (53 sides), the Mills Brothers, Woody Herman, Louis Armstrong, Duke Ellington, Guy Lombardo, Kate Smith, Jimmy Grier, The Dorsey Brothers, Victor Young, Dick McIntire, Lani McIntire & His Hawaiians, John Scott Trotter (Bing's favorite overall), organist Eddie Dunstedter, Matty Malneck, brother Bob Crosby, Carmen Cavallaro, the Ken Darby Singers, Connee Boswell (alone) the Williams Brothers (with Andy Williams), Bob Hope (naturally), Vic Schoen, Louis Jordan & His Tympany Five, Judy Garland, Xavier Cugat, Eddie Haywood, Buddy Cole & His Trio with Mel Tormé & the Meltones, Bob Haggart, Lionel Hampton, Les Paul Trio, Russ Morgan, classical violinist Jascha Heifetz, Fred Waring & the Gleeclub, Sy Oliver, Frank Sinatra, Peggy Lee & Dave Barbour, Glenn Miller, and dozens of guests on his radio show, The Kraft Music Hall, and later on television, and as a guest on many shows over many years.

Bing's Gold

Recordings that sold over one million copies all are Decca recordings except "True Love"

Sweet Leilani	Don't Fence Me In
New San Antonio Rose	I Can't Begin to Tell You
White Christmas	McNamara's Band
Silent Night	South America, Take It Away
Sunday, Monday, or Always	Alexander's Ragtime Band
Pistol Packin' Mama	Whiffenpoof Song
Jingle Bells	Now is the Hour
I'll be Home for Christmas	Galway Bay
Swinging on a Star	Dear Hearts and Gentle People
Too-ra-loo-ra-loo-ral	Play a Simple Melody
Sam's Song	True Love

On June 9, 1960, Decca awarded Bing a platinum disc for his 200 millionth recording sold, then in October 15, 1970, a platinum disc for his 300 millionth. He has topped 400 millions in sales.

White Christmas

BING: "I had something to do with another song, Irving Berlin's 'White Christmas,' which has become a modern Christmas carol by popular acclaim. Every Christmas it booms out of department store loud-speakers over the heads of shoppers and street-corner Santa Clauses. In the trade, 'White Christmas' is known as a standard. Anything heard seasonally is a standard. It's a great song with a simple melody, and nowadays anywhere I go I have to sing it. It's as much a part of me as 'When the Blue of the Night Meets the Gold of the Day' or my floppy ears."

Epilogue: Bing had scheduled a record date at Decca set for his return from Spain. The musicians for the engagement were also booked in advance, and, as tradition had it, they were to be paid whether or not the session took place. This, of course, was due to last-minute cancellations, whereupon musicians would be left without work. When the news of Bing's

The original
Decca 1942
label

Bing's Top Forty Hits

1931 – Out of Nowhere, Just One More Chance, At Your Command
1932 – Dinah (w/Mills Brothers), Please
1933 – Brother Can You Spare a Dime, You're Getting to be a Habit
     with Me, Shadow Waltz
1934 – Little Dutch Mill, Love in Bloom, June in January
1935 – Soon, It's Easy to Remember, Red Sails in the Sunset
1936 – Pennies from Heaven
1937 – Sweet Leilani, Too Marvelous for Words, The Moon Got in
     My Eyes, Remember Me, Bob White (w/Connee Boswell)
1938 – I've Got a Pocketful of Dreams, Alexander's Ragtime Band
     (w/Connee Boswell), You Must Have Been a Beautiful Baby
1940 – Sierra Sue, Trade Winds, Only Forever
1942 – White Christmas
1943 – Moonlight Becomes You, Sunday, Monday or Always
1944 – San Fernando Valley, I Love You, I'll Be seeing You,
     Swinging On a Star, A Hot Time in the Town of Berlin
     (w/Andrews Sisters), Don't Fence Me In (w/Andrews
     Sisters)
1945 – It's Been a Long Long Time, I Can't Begin to Tell You,
1948 – Now is the Hour
1949 – Far Away Places
1950 – Play a Simple Melody(w/Gary)

Bing's Academy Award Winning Songs

"Sweet Leilani" from *Waikiki Wedding* 1937
"White Christmas" from *Holiday Inn* 1942
"Swinging On a Star" from *Going My Way* 1944
"In the Cool, Cool, Cool of the Evening" from *Here Comes the Groom* 1951

passing reached New York, every studio musician refused payment. They all felt they would have played for no pay at all, feeling it a distinct privilege and an honor to play for Bing Crosby.

With thousands of recordings to consider, including air checks and special material, a further reference to Bing's recording history can be found in Bing Crosby's Commercial Recordings compiled by F.B.(Wig) Wiggins in 2001.

Bing and Television

Conquering another medium in stride.

When television moved radio aside, it was a natural for Bing. After all, as Bob Hope once quipped, "...television...you can now go blind in six delicious flavors..and Bing is colorblind."

Bing's television appearances were mostly *specials* on the *Hollywood Palace* show as well as on Bob Hope's TV shows. In 1950 Bing appeared with Perry Como on an ABC special. In 1962 Bing and Bob appeared together on Bob Hope's show celebrating their 30th year in entertainment on NBC. On Bing's *Hollywood Palace* TV Christmas Show in 1968, Kathryn and the children appeared with Bing. Right up until 1977 Bing headlined Christmas shows with his family. In 1971 Bing and Bob made a joint appearance on NBC's "Chrysler Presents the Bob Hope Special." In 1977, the special entitled *Bing* also showcased Bette Midler, who was dressed up as an usher in a comedy role.

Bing actually began his television appearances in 1948 on the *Philco Television Playhouse* on NBC where he sang "Silent Night." The show was kinescoped from studio 9H in New

A Bing Crosby Special with Dean Martin, Frank Sinatra, and Rosemary Clooney
(R. Grudens collection)

York. After appearing on the 1949 show *An Evening with Richard Rodgers*, with Mary Martin and other notable guests, Bing then appeared on *The Red Cross Fund Program* in February of 1951, hosted by Ed Sullivan with Bob Hope and Judy Garland among the guests. Most people document this show as Bing's serious debut. In 1952 Bing, Bob and Dorothy Lamour hosted a telethon for the U.S. Olympic team. It was a simulcast on both NBC and CBS and co-starred Dean Martin and Jerry Lewis, Phil Harris, and Ezio Pinza, who played the lead in Rodgers and Hammerstein's great musical *South Pacific* on Broadway.

On that show, according to *Time Magazine*: "Bing was glibly polysyllabic and seems assured of a lively and profitable TV career whenever he wants it." Bing's reaction: "Well, I guess I'm off and on the road to vaudeville...again."

Bing appeared on hundreds of television shows over the years, frequently as a guest. From the *Paul Anka Show* to the *Rich Little Show*, Bing was always on the tube. There were interviews on morning talk shows about any and all subjects, from his opinions on Broadway shows to exchanges with Johnny Carson and tributes with old friends like songwriter Johnny Mercer.

Already a superstar of immense proportions, television showcased the mature Crosby, but his star had already been cast and his legacy assured. Bing appeared on over 300 telecasts which included 127 of specials in which he starred.

The Bandleaders

Bing performed and recorded with many bands, small groups and large orchestras. These were notable and important to his career:

Paul Whiteman

As noted earlier, it was big band vocalist Mildred Bailey who suggested to "King of Jazz" orchestra leader Paul Whiteman that he investigate performances of an act named Crosby and Rinker, so he sent band members Matty Malneck and Ray Turner to scout out the act. Whiteman was always at the forefront.

Paul Whiteman commenced his band in 1918 at the beautiful Fairmont Hotel in San Francisco, after learning music from his father, who was a music teacher. He had first played violin in the San Francisco Symphony.

In the days when radio was a novelty, television far in the future, and sound films ten years away, it was difficult for a band to become nationally known. Paul Whiteman was lucky. When he recorded "Whispering" and

Paul Whiteman conducts (R. Grudens collection)

"Japanese Sandman" he achieved national prominence. The band had done well in the East, but, thanks to a convention held in Atlantic City, the Victor Phonograph Company salesman heard the orchestra at the Ambassador Hotel and signed them to a recording contract. Heavily promoted, the band and those two tunes became world famous, thanks to recordings that eventually sold millions in a time when there were few phonographs. However, jazz was on everyone's lips. The changes it brought about in popular music caused sensations, and the musicians, black and white, who were caught up in it went on to achieve everlasting fame.

An impressive list of musicians, many who would go on to be future music stars, paraded through Whiteman's great, innovative orchestra: Henry Busse, Ferde Grofe', Matty Malneck, Leon "Bix" Beiderbecke, Frankie "Tram" Trumbauer, Hoagy Carmichael, Eddie Lang, Joe Venuti, Tony Romano (who traveled with Bob Hope's USO troupe), Jack and Charlie Teagarden, Billy Butterfield, Bunny Berigan, Lennie Hayton, Nat Shilkret, Red Nichols, Tommy Dorsey,

1928 JANUARY 20 SALARIES – PAYROLL 3
PAUL WHITEMAN ORCHESTRA
WEEK ENDING JAN.-JAN. 20. 28
MOSQUE THEATRE- NEWARK N.J.

MAYER	RED	sax	"	175	Red Mayer
BARRIS, HARRY		piano	"	150	Harry Barris
BIEDERBECKE, DIX		trumpet	"	200	Bix Beiderbecke
BOUMAN, J.		violin	"	145	J Bouman
BROWN, S.		bass	"	175	S Brown
BUSSE, HENRY		trumpet	"	350	Henry Busse
CROSBY, BING		vocal	"	150	Bing Crosby
CULLEN, B.		trombone	"	150	B.H. Cullen
DIETERLE, K.		violin	"	175	K. Dieterle
DORSEY, JIMMY		sax	"	200	J. Dorsey
FULTON, J.		trombone	"	200	J Fulton
GAYLORD, C.		violin	,	200	C Gaylord
HALL, WILBUR		trombone	"	350	Wilbur Hall
HAZLETT, C.		sax	"	350	C Hazlett
CROZIER, R.		sax	"	175	R Crozier
McDONALD, K.		drums	"	175	John McDonald
McLEAN, HAL		sax	"	200	Hal McLean
MALNECK, MATTY		violin	"	150	M Malneck
MAYHEW, BROS.		sax	"	350	N Mayhew
PERRELLA, H.		piano	"	300	H Perrella
PERRY, MARIO		accordian	"	180	M Perry
PINGITORE, MIKE		banjo	"	300	M. Pingitore
RINKER, AL		piano	"	150	A. Rinker
RUSSELL, M.		violin	"	150	Mischa Russell
SATTERFIELD, Tom		piano	"	150	Tom Satterfield
STRICKFADEN, C.		sax	"	200	C Strickfaden
TRAFFICANTE, MIKE		bass-tuba	"	175	Mike Trafficante
YOUNG, A.		banjo-vocal	"	200	A Young
MARGULIS, C.		trumpet	"	175	C Margulis
GILLESPIE, J.F.		manager	"	350	J F Gillespie
GROFE, FERDE		arranger	"	375	Ferde Grofe
CHALLIS, O.		arranger	"	175	B Challis
LORENZEN, M.		stage	"	110	
BLACK, W.	Wm Black	valet	"	50	
TRAMBAUER FRANK		sax	"	200	F Trumbauer
RANK, W.		trombone	"	200	7440 W Rank

Jimmy Dorsey, arranger Bill Challis, vocalists Al Rinker, Harry Barris, Mildred Bailey, singer and composer Johnny Mercer, and Bing Crosby. Whiteman's theme was George Gershwin's "Rhapsody In Blue." His "Tag Line" was *King of Jazz, Rajah of Rhythm*, and *Monarch of Melody*.

On February 12, 1924, after returning from a successful European tour, Whiteman appeared with his great orchestra at Aeolian Hall in New York to introduce George Gershwin's great jazz composition, "Rhapsody In Blue." George Gershwin himself played the piano that evening. Thirty-four musicians, a group of singers, and arrangers filled the bandstand of this all-star orchestra, helping it to become the biggest name in the music business.

A rotund, portly, and dignified man sporting a thin mustache and a wry smile, Paul Whiteman was the quintessential band leader of the Big Band Era, recording for Victor, Columbia, Decca, Capitol, and Signature labels during his long career. When you met him, and I worked on the fifth floor at NBC in New York as a studio page in the early fifties where I saw him daily and spoke to him often, you knew you were in the company of a grandiose, suave and regal, exalted person of great celebrity. No one can deny Whiteman's contribution to the field of popular jazz music, and as one who championed the welfare of the professional musician. Many feel the absence of Paul Whiteman would have adversely altered the history of the big band business that proliferated throughout the 1920s, '30s, and '40s.

Paul Whiteman was honored by his peers as being named the Dean of Modern American Music. He passed on, a victim of a heart attack, in December, 1967. He was seventy-seven. Bing Crosby made over 100 recordings with Whiteman and always honored their association, which had lasted for over three and a half years.

In Williamstown, Massachusetts, a Paul Whiteman Museum is located at Williams College. It is a worthy trip. Visitors may view and press the keys of the baby grand piano the Rhythm Boys used when they performed "The Bluebirds and the Blackbirds" and the other songs of those golden days. In the vault are the original scores for all of Whiteman's recordings. The hand written notations on actual music sheets used during recording sessions are clearly visible. There are endless scrapbooks of press clippings that followed performances of Bing and the band as they toured, transporting museum-goers back to a time when one could hear things like "Dardenella," that included Bix Beiderbecke playing cornet and the arrangement by the great Bill Challis; or "I'm Comin' Virginia," with Red Nichols on cornet, Jimmy Dorsey on alto sax, Eddie Lang on his jazz guitar, and Bing on vocal.

Upon the death of Paul Whiteman in December of 1967, John S. Wilson of the New York Times wrote, *"Although Mr. Whiteman's relationship to jazz was more talk than fact, he was a great catalytic force in other areas of American music in the Twenties. He was a groundbreaker — a pioneer whose imagination and showmanship moved popular music in directions that are still developing today."*

Gus Arnheim — Learning His Craft

For Bing Crosby, it was his affiliation with Gus Arnheim's Cocoanut Grove Band that jump-started his solo singing career. Formerly a piano player with Abe Lyman's Orchestra, Gus Arnheim started his own band in 1926 at the nationally famous Cocoanut Grove night club located in the Los Angeles Ambassador Hotel, where they broadcast their music for two hours each night over a coast-to-coast radio hookup. Among his vocalists were Andy Russell, who doubled on drums; Shirley Ross; (remember her sharing vocals with Bob Hope's "Thanks for the Memory" in the film *The Big Broadcast of 1938*); and Russ Columbo, whose singing career paralleled Bing's.

Bing has profoundly credited Gus Arnheim as one of the major contributors to his success. The solo recording with Arnheim that brought Bing national recognition was "Out of Nowhere," and it attained the number one position on the music charts. Bing singing on Arnheim's recordings "Wrap Your Troubles in Dreams" and "Just a Gigolo" brought Bing extended fame. It was Arnheim's 1931 recording of Harry Barris' "I Surrender Dear" that brought Bing into national prominence, leading to his own radio show on CBS.

Arnheim's band frequently toured the entire country and performed in two European tours with his fourteen piece band

and female vocalist. They performed in ballrooms, dance pavilions, hotels, and theaters.

After World War II, Arnheim disbanded, taking up film writing in Hollywood. He passed on in January 1955 of a heart attack at the young age of fifty-six.

John Scott Trotter — Best of the Best

The familiar musical sounds of John Scott Trotter's orchestra are closely and unequivocally identified with Bing Crosby's recordings of the 1930s and beyond. Beginning with "It's the Natural Thing to Do," on July 12, 1937 and on the "B" side "The Moon Got in My Eyes," followed by "Smarty," Trotter and Crosby continued to record together for over seventeen productive years.

It was about this time Bing began recording duets with Connee Boswell, one third of the popular Boswell Sisters, starting with "Basin Street Blues." Some of Bing's choice recordings with John Scott Trotter were "My Heart is Taking Lessons," "This is My Night to Dream," "On the Sentimental Side," "You're a Sweet Little Headache," and "The Folks Who Live on the Hill." Bing and John Scott were cranking them out to that special Bing and Trotter sound week by week.

....
John Scott Trotter, Ethel Merman and Bing
(R. Grudens collection)
....

Trotter, who began his career playing piano and arranging in the band of Hal Kemp when Bing first knew him, left New York in 1936 to camp out with songwriter Johnny Burke on the West Coast. He rediscovered Bing, and eventually became his principal musical director and began working on Bing's *Kraft Music Hall* radio program in June of 1937.

On June 1, 1937, John Scott received a telegram from Bing and Larry Crosby: "CAN YOU BE HERE 21ST. DORSEY LEAVING. YOU'RE TO TAKE OVER MUSIC ON KRAFT SHOW."

On June 21, John Scott walked in Larry Crosby's office, said hello to Bing, and a few minutes later left for his summer vacation. He was permanently set as the *Kraft Music Hall* musical director.

When the show with John Scott got under way, he was amazed how Bing would go through his rehearsals so casually, break off and make conversation with others with a wink and a smile, and yet complete the necessary revelations of rehearsals. John Scott figured what Bing's low note was. He eventually found the range that was most comfortable for him, which turned out to be G to C.

Trotter's swinging, lilting, sweet, yet staccato style arrangements complimented Bing's phrasing and timing, car-

John Scott
Trotter's
birthday
*(K. Crosby
collection)*

rying him along beautifully on tunes like "Hang Your Heart on a Hickory Limb," "That Sly Old Gentleman," Swinging On a Star," "If I Had My Way," and "Wrap Your Troubles in Dreams." The songs were true Crosby evergreens that set a special style through Trotter's unique arrangements.

WRAP YOUR TROUBLES IN DREAMS
Ted Koehler, Billy Moll, and Harry Barris

When skies are cloudy and gray
They're only gray for a day,
So wrap your troubles in dreams,
And dream your troubles away,
Until that sunshine peeps through,
There's only one thing to do,
Just wrap your troubles in dreams,
And dream your troubles away.
Castles may tumble
That's fate after all,
Life's very funny that way...
No use to grumble
Just smile as they fall,
Weren't you King for a day?
Just remember that sunshine,
Always follows the rain,
So wrap your troubles in dreams
And dream your troubles away.

Bing said, "Trotter is a real gourmet, dedicated to the pleasures of the table. He follows food the way some people follow the sun."

Trotter would fly from Los Angeles to New Orleans just for the joy of eating Oyster's Rockefeller at famous Antoine's Restaurant, then back again in time for a radio show appearance with Bing. He was a bachelor who cooked and learned by necessity. He made weird combinations of food and even prepared his own ice cream, using the exact, proper ingredients. John Scott weighed just under three hundred pounds. He was a person with an amazing amount of self-control when conducting. Raising his voice was a rarity, even when everything went awry on a recording date. He never resorted to profanity during stress periods with musicians, of which there were many.

Kathryn Crosby liked John Scott Trotter, who, it was said, was a loner involved in acquiring antiques and preparing terrific meals. A serious collector, in the 1950s he and his sister Margaret once owned an antique shop in Laguna, Virginia. He was president of an Antiques Dealers Association. John Scott never married or ever kept company, as far as anyone knows.

"The kids loved John Scott," said Kathryn. He and Bing became lasting friends. Everybody liked him. A virtual musical genius who knew many musicians and just how to deal effectively with them, John Scott hired young Nelson Riddle and bandleader/arranger Billy May, and allowed them to take over his arranging chores. Later, they each became music icons of their own, especially on Frank Sinatra recording dates.

In 1954, Gary Crosby substituted for his Dad on a radio show sponsored by General Electric. The show ran for 13 weeks. Bing wrote to John Scott about the show, saying he enjoyed it and telling him he also liked his arrangements. He was concerned about Gary's delivery, feeling his voice production was weak and needed reinforcement by practicing daily. He suggested certain songs he felt Gary could handle more easily. Bing's concern for Gary's success was further proof of his fatherly interest, this time working through his musical director John Scott Trotter.

John Scott Trotter passed on in 1975 at the age of sixty-seven, two years before Bing. He had conducted the music for more Bing Crosby recordings than any other bandleader.

Glenn Miller

In 1929 Glenn Miller recorded a dozen or so sides with the Dorsey Brothers Orchestra. Some of those recordings featured an up-and-coming singer who loved to hang around jazz musicians. It was Bing Crosby. The songs were "The Spell of the Blues," Let's Do It" and "My Kinda Love." It was Glenn's idea to pitch the brass down to Bing's register. So, instead of the usual couple of trumpets and just one trombone, Glenn featured three trombones, Tommy, Glenn and Don Novis, and just one trumpet, Bunny Berigan.

Bing was connected to the great Glenn Miller over many years. When Glenn applied for a job with the Air Force at the beginning of the war, Bing sent a letter praising the bandleader.

"It is a great privilege for me to make the recommendation for whatever it is worth, as in the many years I've known Mr. Miller, I've found him to be a very high type young man, full of resourcefulness, adequately intelligent and a suitable type to command men or assist in organization."

When Bing was touring Europe for the USO, entertaining the troops, he joined up with the Miller band in England, and on August 30, 1944 sang in a recording session. Because of the shortage of metal, the recordings were not preserved. Instead, they were scrapped after being used for broadcasts to the troops so that the metal discs could be recoated for future shows.

Glenn Miller, 1940 *(R. Grudens collection)*

Crosby was very impressed with the fine musicians in the band. After the session was over, Bing took off a hand-painted tie he was wearing and autographed it to "Glenn Miller's AAF Band — the Greatest Thing Since the Invention of Cup Mutes!"

The boys were mutually impressed with Bing's lack of formality, a contrast to Glenn Miller's usual disciplined attitude. The band members took home fond memories of the Crosby session. Bing had brought some Scotch and other whiskey for the boys. It was said that they recorded some of the best material the band ever played that day.

BING: "We had amusing incidents in England. Glenn and I were dining in Soho and a crowd grew and demanded I sing and then only would they disperse, because there was a law in effect that because of the bombings no groups were allowed to assemble in the streets.

"I asked them to disperse if I sang 'Pennies from Heaven.' I did and they did.

"A fog came in that night, I remember, and we had to crawl back to our hotel about a mile on our hands and knees, feeling the curb as we moved along.

"I was going over to France in a day or so, and Glenn offered to send Jack Russin, his pianist, over to expand my

Bing Crosby

Hollywood

'June 22, 1942

To Whom It May Concern:

Mr. Glenn Miller advises me
that there's a possibility of his being
selected for training, with the ultimate
result a commission in the United States
Navy, and that he is desirous of securing
letters of recommendation from friends
of his that might be of some value.

It is a great privilege for
me to make this recommendation for whatever it is worth, as in the many years
I've known Mr. Miller I've found him to
be a very high type young man, full of
resourcefulness, adequately intelligent
and a suitable type to command men or
assist in organization.

Bing Crosby

Bing Crosby

accompaniment. He left on a later plane, and though he got to France, we never did get together. I think Jack had a marvelous time, touring around France, looking for me, and visiting the various pubs and military installations.

The Songwriters

Without the songwriters, would Bing have been a lawyer?

Who were the great Crosby songwriters? Did they write songs just for him, or just compose random tunes that Bing either discovered or were brought to his attention by musicians or record producers? Did Bing write some of his own tunes?

Bing recommending Glenn Miller to the Navy, 1942 (G. Simon collection)

Johnny Mercer

According to Johnny Mercer, he first took notice of Bing when he first heard the old recordings "Wistful and Blue" and "Old Man River" with Paul Whiteman. "My admiration has remained undiminished ever since. It was Bing's recording of my song 'I'm An Old Cowhand' that opened doors in Hollywood for me." Looking back, Johnny Mercer and Bing Crosby were originally a couple of cut-ups singers who got their start with Paul Whiteman's Orchestra.

Mercer entered Paul Whiteman's "Youth of America" contest for unknown singers, and in 1933 organized a trio for a radio broadcast, remaining with the organization for three years serving as vocalist, songwriter, emcee and special material writer.

By 1939 Bing had developed a close association with Savannah, Georgia born Mercer and his wife, Ginger, an earlier friend of Bing. At one time, when Bing lived in Hollywood and Mercer resided on East 60th Street in New York City, the two found convenience in regularly exchanging mail rather than utilizing the telephone, as they could never get one another on the phone. Although Johnny Mercer generally wrote lyrics, alone or in association with others, he also composed much of his own music, and was a pretty decent singer himself. Bing sang many Mercer tunes so there was always something for the two to work on or talk about.

Later on, after establishing a successful songwriting career in Tin Pan Alley, Broadway and motion pictures, with the help of librettist lyricist Buddy DeSylva's financing, (he wrote "April Showers" for Jolson) Mercer formed Capitol Records with his partner Glen Wallichs, the owner of a Hollywood music store.

Mercer penned the lyrics to Harold Arlen's music for "*Star Spangled Rhythm*," a film featuring everyone on the Paramount Pictures roster, most in cameo roles. Bing sang Mercer's "That Old Black Magic" and "Old Glory" in that film. Bing recorded many Mercer tunes along his path to success: "Jeepers, Creepers," "Ac-Cent-Tchu-Ate the Positive," "Blues in the Night," "Bob White,", "Welcome Stranger," "I'm An Old Cowhand," "In the Cool, Cool, Cool of the Evening," "Lazy Bones," "Mr. Meadowlark," "You Must Have Been a Beautiful Baby, and "Dearly Beloved."

DEARLY BELOVED

Johnny Mercer and Jerome Kern

Dearly beloved, how clearly I see,
Somewhere in Heaven you were fashioned for me,
Angel eyes knew you,
Angel voices led me to you;
Nothing could save me, Fate gave me a sign;
I know that I'll be yours come shower or shine;
So I say merely,
Dearly beloved, be mine.

Mercer won four Oscars, and had fourteen of his songs achieve number one on *Your Hit Parade* radio program. He wrote about 1,500 songs for more than 70 films and seven Broadway musicals; many have become standards.

Johnny Mercer also sang his own tunes from time to time. His versions of "Laura," "Mr. Meadowlark" and "Tangerine" suited him and his singing well. When he performed on the *Chesterfield Radio Program* as a 1944 summer replacement for Bob Hope's Pepsodent show, some thought he was a black

Bing Crosby
—Hollywood—

April 13, 1939

Dear "Verseable":

I thought you would be out this way afore now
and was surprised to learn you're not coming for a piece.
We all miss your Saturday nite insouciance, but of course
you should strike while the iron is hot - and you've got
it good and hot right now.

"Angels," to my way of thinking, is your best
lyric to date. You're getting practically poetic. It's
a hunk of song. Trouble is, by the time Kapp gets them
to me, all the good singers have opened many lengths on
me.

I hope you kept Drinkable out of the clip joints
during his Gotham Sabbatical. Doesn't take but two flagons
of Trommers' Lager to send him on the town.

Laughable is a champion now. He's at Palm
Springs with his ma, catching a tan and getting well
spoiled by all the ladies. He slays the chickadees.
Strictly a Crosby, I guess.

"Eastside of Heaven" was good fun under the
expansive aegis of D. Wingate Butler. Never engaged in
a more pleasant and, I hope, profitable enterprise. The
budget was astonishingly low and, if John Public takes to
the picture favorably, we're a cinch to make a meg or two.

Now, John, we're expecting you here for the
racing and the 'surfin' and turfin', so pack up Ginger
et al and summer out this way.

Your friend,

Bing

Mr. John Mercer
111 E. 60th.
New York, New York

singer because of his deep Southern accent. He actually received a post card from the *Abraham Lincoln Junior Club of Chicago*, informing him that he was voted "the most popular young colored singer on the radio." Bing's duet with Mercer on "Small Fry" is one of Bing's classics.

Bing Crosby and Johnny Mercer formed an early, unbroken lifelong friendship.

Johnny Mercer: "The interesting part of Bing to me is that he likes to be with the jockeys, with millionaires, with beach boys and caddies. He liked colorful people; he likes people who are amusing and who aren't phonies. He's an unphony man. He's so distant, but he's genuine."

I'M AN OLD COWHAND
Johnny Mercer

*I'm an old cowhand from the Rio Grande
But my legs ain't bowed and my cheeks ain't tanned,
I'm a cowboy who never saw a cow,
Never roped a steer 'cause I don't know how,
And I sho' ain't fix-in' to start in now
Yip-py I-O-Ki-Ay
I'm an old cowhand from the Rio Grande,
And I learned to ride 'fore I learned to stand,
I'm a ridin' fool who is up to date,
I know every trail in the Lone Star State,
'Cause I ride the range in a Ford V Eight
Yip-py I O-Ki-Ay
I'm an old cowhand from the Rio Grande,
And I come to town just to hear the band,
I know all the songs that the cowboys know,
'Bout the big corral where the doagies go,
'Cause I learned them all on the radio.
Yip-py I-O-Ki-Ay
I'm an old cowhand from the Rio Grande
Where the West is wild 'round the Borderland
Where the buffalo roam around the zoo,
And the Indians make you a rug or two,
And the old Bar X is a Bar-B-Q,
Yip-py-I-O-Ki-Ay
Yip-py I-O-Ki-Ay*

"I'm An Old Cowhand"

Jimmy Van Heusen and Johnny Burke

Composer Jimmy Van Heusen collaborated with lyricist Johnny Burke in the 1940s, and they became the two songwriters mostly identified with Bing Crosby.

The team produced many of their best songs just for him: "The Bells of St. Mary's," "Swinging on a Star," "Moonlight Becomes You," "Sunday, Monday, or Always," "Aren't You Glad You're You," and "Once and for Always" a song Bing shared with beautiful Rhonda Fleming in the lavish musical *A Connecticut Yankee in King Arthur's Court*.

Jimmy's original name was Edward Chester Babcock. It was totally replaced when he applied for a job with radio station WSYR and the manager insisted he change it. An advertisement noticed for popular Van Heusen shirts did the trick, coupled with the natural sounding prefix Jimmy, and he got the job. He never, however, legally changed his name.

Before he composed for Bing, Van Heusen wrote "Imagination," which was introduced by the classy orchestra and chorus of Fred Waring's Pennsylvanians. After the team of Burke and Van Heusen migrated to Hollywood, they worked a few movies with uncelebrated tunes until they were contracted to compose the songs for the first Paramount "Road" picture, *Road to Singapore*. Bing had insisted the song writing team produce the songs for that film. The collaboration of Crosby with Jimmy Van Heusen and Johnny Burke lasted a long ten years, and included this wonderful song from Bing's Oscar winning film *Going My Way*.

....
L to R.
Jimmy Van Heusen and Johnny Burke
(R. Grudens collection)
....

GOING MY WAY

Johnny Burke & Jimmy Van Heusen

Good morning friend.
It's certainly a pleasant time to walk,
So fresh and green and clear and bright
I'm looking for some company
Thought maybe we could talk
Do you go left or right?
(refrain)
This road leads to Rainbowville
Going my way?
Up ahead is Bluebird Hill
Going my way?
Just pack a basket full of wishes
And off you start with Sunday morning in your heart
'Round the bend you'll see a sign
"Dreamer's Highway."
Happiness is down the line
Going my way?
The smiles you'll gather will look well on you
Oh, I hope you're going my way too.

Lyricist Johnny Burke, unlike his partner, retained his own name, being born in Antioch, California in 1908. At five years old, Johnny emigrated to Chicago with his family and took up piano and dramatic acting, and eventually was hired as a piano demonstrator for the firm of Irving Berlin, Inc., moving on to New York to work for their East Coast office. His first successful lyrics were "Annie Doesn't Live Here Anymore" introduced by and for the Fred Waring Orchestra. He collaborated with Arthur Johnston on the film *Pennies from Heaven*, a Columbia Pictures film in which Bing appeared while on loan from Paramount.

"When we do a song, people don't say that it's a typical Burke-Van Heusen song. Instead, they say it's a typical Crosby song. I am proud of that."

The challenge to write a song about a priest who was lecturing a gang of wayward juveniles about honoring the *Ten Commandments*, for a film entitled *Going My Way*, Johnny was struck by a phrase while having dinner at the home of Bing Crosby, when Bing admonished one of his kids, declaring,

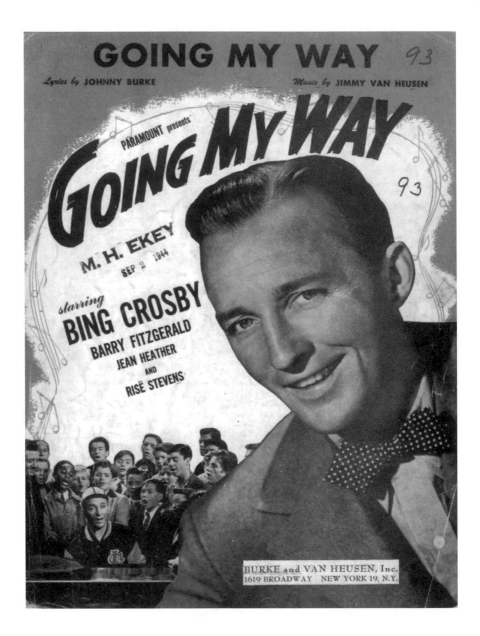

"....you're acting just like a mule." Burke picked up on it, wondering what an unruly child would be like if he behaved as a fish... or a pig. By the following morning, the lyrics were committed to a lead sheet. It was eventually named "Swinging on a Star" to which Johnny Van Heusen added his music. The song, as well as the film, won the Academy Award in 1944:

SWINGING ON A STAR
Johnny Burke and Jimmy Van Heusen

Would you like to swing on a star
Carry moonbeams home in a jar
And be better off than you are,
Or would you rather be a mule?

A mule is an animal with long funny ears,
He kicks up at anything he hears,
His back is brawny and his brain is weak,
He's just plain stupid with a stubborn streak,
And by the way if you hate to go to school
You may grow up to be a mule
Or would you rather swing on a star,
Carry moonbeams home in a jar
And be better off than you are
Or would you rather be a pig?

A pig is an animal with dirt on his face,
His shoes are a terrible disgrace,
He's got no manners when he eats his food,
He's fat and lazy and extremely rude,
But if you don't care a feather or a fig,
You may grow up to be a pig.
Or would you rather be a fish?

A fish won't do anything but swim in a brook,
He can't write his name or read a book
To fool the people is his only thought,
And though he's slippery, he still gets caught.
But then if that sort of life is what you wish
You may grow up to be a fish

And all the monkeys aren't in the zoo
Every day you meet quite a few
So, you see, it's all up to you
You can be better than you are
You could be swinging on a star.

The Burke-Van Heusen songs from the movie *Welcome Stranger* are particularly pleasant: "As Long as I'm Dreaming," "Smile Right Back at the Sun," and "My Heart is a Hobo", Bing executing them perfectly. And, how about the rambling ditty "Sunshine Cake" that Bing reveled in with pretty Colleen Gray in the stables of the film *Riding High*?

The prolific team wrote many songs without the benefit of Bing's performances. Frank Sinatra evergreens "Pocketful of Miracles," "The Second Time Around," "My Kind of Town," "Come Fly with Me," and "All the Way" are just a few. Johnny Burke, while coupled with James Monaco, furnished Bing with "I've Got a Pocketful of Dreams," "Only Forever" and "That's for Me" from the film *Rhythm on the River*.

I've always wondered what course the singing career of Bing Crosby would've taken without the James Van Heusen — Johnny Burke collaboration, or all the great songwriters efforts.

Thank goodness for the songwriters, Bing must have thought. Bing recorded 80 Burke & Van Heusen compositions.

I'VE GOT A POCKETFUL OF DREAMS
Johnny Burke and James V. Monaco

Happiness comes with success
And that I guess is true.
But success is more or less a point of view
(Chorus)
I'm no millionaire
But I'm not the type to care
'Cause I've got a pocketful of dreams
It's my universe
Even with an empty purse
'Cause I've got a pocketful of dreams
Wouldn't take the wealth on Wall Street
For a road where nature trods
And I calculate I'm worth my weight in goldenrod's
Lucky, lucky me
I can live in luxury
'Cause I've got a pocketful of dreams.

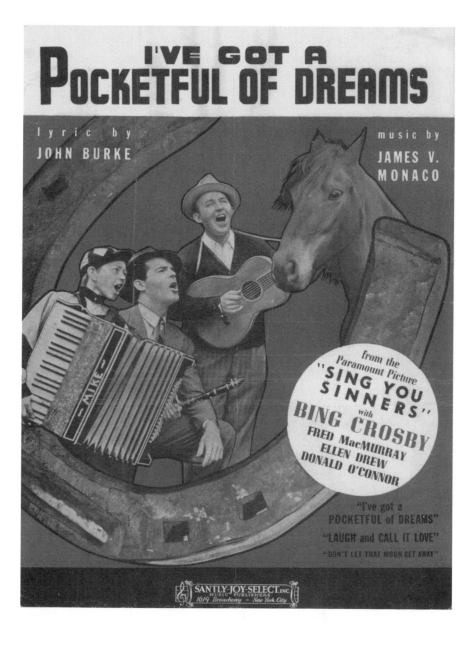

Leo Robin and Ralph Rainger

"Love in Bloom," from the motion picture *She Loves Me Not*, "June in January," from Paramount's *Here Is My Heart* (it was Bing's first recording for Decca), and "Please" from *The Big Broadcast*, were three important songs identified with Bing Crosby. All were written by the songwriting team of Leo Robin and Ralph Rainger.

PLEASE
Leo Robin and Ralph Rainger

Please — lend your little ear to my plea's,
Lend a ray of cheer to my plea's
Tell me that you love me too.
Please — let me hold you tight in my arms,
I could find delight in your charms,
Every night my whole life through
Your eyes reveal that you have the soul of
An angel, white as snow;
How long must I play the role of a gloomy Romeo?
Oh! Please — say you're not intending to tease.
Speed the happy ending and please
Tell me that you love me too.

Leo Robin, born and raised in Pittsburgh, where he studied law, became a professional songwriter instead. After a few small successes, he went to Hollywood in 1928 to write songs for films, working at first with Margaret Whiting's dad, Richard Whiting, on their first composition for French entertainer Maurice Chevalier, entitled "Louise," achieving much success.

With Ralph Rainger, Leo Robin collaborated on some notable Bing Crosby evergreens: "With Every Breath I Take," "You're a Sweet Little Headache," from *Paris Honeymoon*, and "Blue Hawaii," from *Waikiki Wedding*.

Originally a New Yorker, Ralph Rainger began playing piano at age seven. Upon moving to Newark, New Jersey, he began playing in a jazz orchestra at school dances, eventually becoming an attorney. He later turned his back on law to play piano professionally in Broadway shows. His composition "Moanin' Low" was interpolated into a Humphrey Bogart-Lauren Bacall film *Key Largo*, and Harry James performed it in *Young Man With a Horn*, re-creating the role of famed cor-

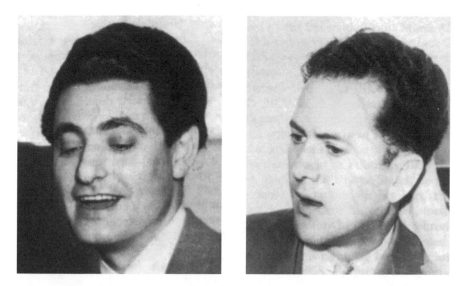

netist Bix Biederbecke in a stirring biography, co-starring vocalist/actress Doris Day.

Rainger followed Leo Robin by two years in emigrating to Hollywood to write for film musicals. Rainger composed the Oscar winning song "Thanks for the Memory," Bob Hope's famous theme, first performed with Shirley Ross in *The Big Broadcast of 1938*, and featured in my 2002 book "The Spirit of Bob Hope."

The magnificent career of Ralph Rainger came to a sudden end in 1942 when he died in an airplane accident near Palm Springs, California.

L to R.
Leo Robin and Ralph Rainger
(R. Grudens collection)

Irving Berlin

"Irving Berlin has no place in American music; he is American music."

So composer Jerome Kern evaluated the *other* master song writer of the twentieth century. Bing had recorded many of Berlin's songs over his career, more than any other composer. In 1911, Irving Berlin wrote one of his most famous songs, "Alexander's Ragtime Band." In his day Berlin was the song writing sensation of *Tin Pan Alley*.

Berlin's invention of melodies of simple charm were written synchronously — that is, music and lyrics together. He

Bing and
Irving Berlin
(R. Grudens
collection)

never had theories about music, he only knew how to write popular songs that readily earned instantaneous public acceptance. His ability to write war songs was phenomenal in itself: "God Bless America," "Any Bonds Today," "Angels of Mercy," "I Left My Heart at the Stage Door Canteen," "This is the Army," and "Oh, How I Hate to Get Up in the Morning" are classics. "God Bless America" was made famous by the singer Kate Smith, and continues on today through the events of September 11, 2001 and is still played today as its symbol. It is known as America's second national anthem.

Irving Berlin, his wife Ellin, and their three daughters, never lived in sumptuous homes, but in only apartments maintained in Hollywood and Gracie Square in New York, as well as on a neat little farm in Livingston Manor, New York. Some of Bing's other recordings of Berlin tunes were: "Now It Can Be Told," "White Christmas," "Count Your Blessings," "Alexander's Ragtime Band," "Blue Skies," "Easter Parade," and "You Keep Coming Back Like a Song."

Berlin composed the music and words for the immensely popular Broadway show *Annie Get Your Gun*, which featured the song "There's No Business Like Show Business," the unofficial anthem of the American Theater.

Interesting thing about Berlin. He had very little musical training and could only play the piano in the key of F-sharp major — by ear. But he utilized a special lever under his piano that transposed any music he played to the desired key.

Irving Berlin is considered to be one of America's most gifted song writers and lived to the age of 100 years.

Anatomy of a Movie
Holiday Inn

One late January night in Washington, D.C., Irving Berlin and Paramount director-producer Mark Sandrich, who had both come from attending a show, sat together in a late-night restaurant talking over an idea for a motion picture story that would bring together a number of songs Berlin had written that featured nationally observed holidays.

Sandrich had been on the lookout for such a novel idea for some time, so the two pieced together a story that would show-case all those songs.

Berlin went home excited that night, worked out a synopsis and named the story *Holiday Inn*, whereupon Sandrich turned it over to five different writers who collectively worked up a suitable screen play.

The story involved characters Jim Hardy (Bing Crosby), Ted Hanover (Fred Astaire) and Lila Dixon (Virginia Dale) — a New York dance trio. Tired and worn, Jim decides the grind is too much for him. He aims to get away from grueling nightclubs and settle down on a farm in Connecticut. Hanover and Dixon reject his idea, preferring the life of penthouses, jewelry, fame and fortune. Featured too were Walter Abel; one of the original Rhythm Boys, Harry Barris; and Bob Crosby's Bobcats.

Jim goes to Connecticut and opens Holiday Inn — open only on holidays — leaving 350 days open for him to loaf and enjoy life on his rural farm. Linda Mason (Marjorie Reynolds) is engaged sight unseen by Jim to appear at his Holiday Inn. Romance develops between them. Jim gets to warble "White Christmas" sitting at a piano in front of a Christmas tree, and Linda joins in, learning the lyrics on the spot, (her voice was actually that of Martha Mears) thus introducing Irving Berlin's best known holiday song to the world and conveying everlasting fame to Bing Crosby for that performance alone.

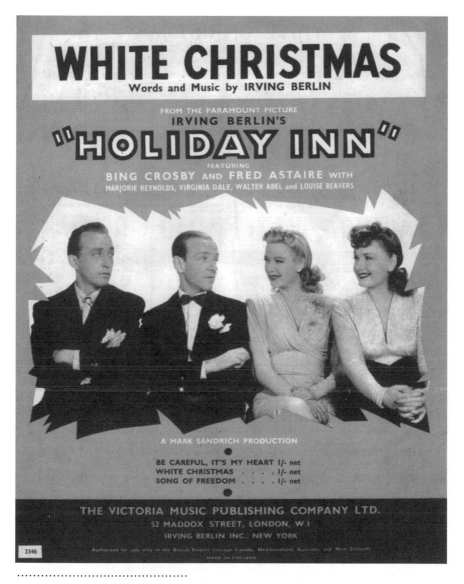

Holiday Inn sheet music from England
(R. Grudens collection)

The song, "White Christmas," won the Academy Award that year, and Irving Berlin was nominated for Best Writing (Original Story) for this classic film. "White Christmas" is a deceptively simple tune, yet a masterpiece of sorts as it surfaces each Christmas season evoking mythical memories which for some people have existed for a lifetime of Christmases. This is one of Bing's best films.

WHITE CHRISTMAS
Irving Berlin

The sun is shining, the grass is green
The orange and palm trees sway
There's never been such a day
In Beverly Hills, L.A.
But it's December, the twenty-fourth
And I am longing to be up North
I'm dreaming of a White Christmas
Just like the ones I used to know
Where the treetops glisten
And children listen
To hear sleigh bells in the snow
I'm dreaming of a White Christmas
With every Christmas card I write
"May your days be merry and bright
And may all your Christmases be white."

....
Bing and Marjorie Reynolds singing original version of "White Christmas" in *Holiday Inn,* 1942 *(courtesy Paramount)*
....

1942

U.S.A.

FILM MUSICAL

L'AMOUR CHANTE ET DANSE
HOLIDAY INN

RÉALISATEUR
Mark Sandrich

French promotion for *Holiday Inn*, 1942
(courtesy Paramount)

At last tired and bored, Lila runs off with another man. Ted is left alone. Ted appears at Jim's Holiday Inn, and tries to woo Linda Mason away from Holiday Inn after dancing with her when under the influence. Jim tries to hide Linda from Ted, but is eventually unsuccessful, although Lillie re-appears as a temporary menace to the Jim-Linda -Ted setup. The story ends happily (of course) for everybody, with Hollywood contracts awarded to everyone. Bing gets the girl and Fred is the loser, displaying to good effect his own vulnerability. Ted (Astaire) finales with Lila and Jim(Crosby) with Linda (Reynolds) and Bing goes Hollywood, too. Why not? Anything can happen in a Hollywood movie.

The glittering film turns out to be tuneful, light-hearted, extremely pleasant entertainment laced with terrific Irving Berlin songs. With Holiday Inn, Bing makes his first film dancing with Fred Astaire. The musicians were John Scott Trotter and His Orchestra, Bob Crosby and His Orchestra, The Music Maids and Hal, and The Ken Darby Singers:

The Songs of Holiday Inn

"Happy Holidays," "Be Careful, It's My Heart," "Abraham, Easter Parade," "I've Got Plenty to Be Thankful For," "Song of Freedom," "I'll Capture Your Heart," "Lazy," "You're Easy to Dance With," "I Can't Tell a Lie," "White Christmas," "Say It with Firecrakers," "Let's Start the New Year Right."

Holiday Inn was one of the best musical films ever, achieving great popularity with Crosby and Astaire fans. Their chemistry sparks the film throughout and the sets are very imaginative. The scenic designs were stunning and realistic, the dance sequences were memorable and the photography was very effectively produced. The premiere of the film at the New York Paramount was held for the Benefit for Navy Relief Society on August 4, 1942. Bing had premiered the song "White Christmas" on his radio program on December 25, 1941, a full seven months before the release of the film.

Anatomy of a Movie
If I Had My Way

When on loan to Universal from Paramount in 1940, one of Bing's most charming movies, *If I Had My Way*, tugs at your heartstrings. The charm was spread by the fine singing voice and the sweet personality of a very young fourteen year old singer named Gloria Jean, who was a co-star, as Bing always insisted, rather than just a featured player. Supporting players were Charles Winninger, the character actor El Brendel, and Allyn Joslyn, in a neat little film filled with snappy vaudeville patter and a host of songs and dances performed by a handful of genuine vaudeville performers.

The songs by Johnny Burke and James Monaco were "I Haven't Got Time to Be a Millionaire;" the very charming song that Bing duets with Gloria Jean "Meet the Sun Halfway;" the thoughtful, musing "If I Had My Way"(one of Bing's best), written by Lou Klein and James Kendis; "April Played the Fiddle," a kind of forced and corny tune; and "Pessimistic Character," a novelty tune.

Bing helped finance the film.

The Story: A construction worker (Bing) takes charge of the daughter of one of his co-workers who was killed while working on a bridge. Bing and his friend, played by Brendel, take the youngster (Gloria Jean) East to find her jovial great uncle (Charles Winninger).

When they arrive in New York they find the uncle, who greets her happily. Bing's friend buys a restaurant that has fallen on hard times, but Bing transforms it into a high-type nightclub that goes on to success so they can restore the money they spent that was supposed have been kept in trust for her education. The script is lightweight, but Bing and Gloria save it all with their great performances: Bing with his enriched baritone and Gloria with her youthful and perfect soprano voice.

The film actually returned the Crosby variety shows to their true origin, vaudeville, as the film seemed to be an attempt by Universal to market-test the appeal of resurrected vaudevillians. In her book, The Pyramid Illustrated *History of the Movies-Bing Crosby*, author Barbara Bauer states: "The film added such ingredients as a Little Orphan Annie plot, El Brendel's Swedish-American stereotype, and the cornball populism that audiences had loved a few years before in *You Can't Take It With You* (snobbish, unfeeling rich people vs. the good-hearted poor people)."

Despite the critical reviews of this lightweight film, I consider the film to be, subjectively, sentimental and enjoyable, with Bing and Gloria Jean singing at their best.

IF I HAD MY WAY
Louis Klein and James Kendis

I'd like to make your golden dream come true, dear
If I only had my way
A paradise this world would seem to you, dear
If I only had my way
If I had my way, dear
Forever there'd be
A garden of roses for you and for me
A thousand and one things, dear
I would do
Just for you, just for you, only you
If I had my way,
We would never grow old
And sunshine I'd bring every day
You would reign all alone
Like a queen on a throne
If I had my way.

In September 2002, Gloria Jean recalls her role with Bing in the film:

"Bing was something else. Not only was he fun to work with, but he really would take a genuine interest in everything that I did. I was only fourteen and he was wary of people who talked to me in interviews, being very protective, like a true dad would be. He always gave me very good advice. Once, he said: ' The one thing that is most important in your life — you must remember it always — no matter how famous you get or how much money you earn — is your family. In this industry, as you get older, your family will become more important to you." And he was so right."

At the time, with Bing's own four boys whom he consciously protected from the press and the public, he worried about Gloria Jean too, being protective because of her youth and being openly exposed to a sometime negatively influential world.

"Bing nor I could read music, but if we heard something just once, why, we were able to sing it with little rehearsal," she explained about successfully performing the songs in the film when they cross-harmonized so beautifully. Gloria would carefully watch Bing, then imitate his phrasing and imitate his contagious and outgoing stage presence. My favorite song in

Sheet music "If I Had My Way" 1940
(G. Jean collection)

Left: Bing and
Gloria Jean
Bottom: Bing,
Gloria Jean and
Charles
Winninger, 1940
*(courtesy Gloria
Jean)*

the film was 'I Haven't the Time to Be a Millionaire.'

"Bing and I sang together all the time. His voice was so light and rich. Our voices blended very, very well. Bing had a carefree style of singing, and he let me be myself, so it worked well. I loved singing with him more than anyone ever in my career.

"And Bing was a cutup, too, always a lot of fun on the set. He made everything light and easy, always kidding around. Singing on

Singing with Gloria Jean and El Brendel– "I Haven't the Time to Be a Millionaire" *(courtesy Universal Studios)*

his radio shows it was the same thing, easy and fun to do. Bing would put the radio audience at ease just by his presence — and with no pretensions. I adored Bing. I have never met his wife Kathryn, but I can tell that I would like her. I've never known anyone since like Bing Crosby, have you?"

Gloria Jean obviously enjoyed singing and acting in films of which there were over twenty-five during her seven year contract at Universal, working with some of the greatest stars: Groucho Marx, W.C. Fields, Noah Berry, Allan Jones, Donald O'Connor, Woody Herman, Bob Crosby, Olsen & Johnson, The Andrews Sisters, Carmen Miranda, Bob Hope, and many more.

"In my retirement, I live by the ocean in California with my sister Bonnie. My son Angelo has three daughters and they are the joy of my life. The three little girls are pure heaven. Clara is six, Julia is seven, and the baby is seven months old I'm very proud to have been part of the golden age of films and music. I have retained many wonderful memories. And singing with Bing made it even more memorable and beautiful."

Bob Hope, Les Paul, Rosemary Clooney, Louis Armstrong James Cagney, Rhonda Fleming, Patty Andrews, Phil Harris, Tony Bennett, Jack Benny, Peggy Lee, Mel Tormé, Fred Astaire, Jack Ellsworth, The Mills Brothers, Mary Martin, Joe Franklin, Connie Haines, Jerry Vale, Frankie Laine and Sally Bennett

Bob and Bing and the Road Pictures

"When you work with Bing, you always look great."

BING: "Sorry I'm late, Bob. I had trouble finding a place to park."

BOB: "What do you mean? The stable's right outside."

BING: "Is that what that was? I thought it was your dressing room. It was — the last time I was on your show."

Remember the comedy teams of Burns and Allen, Abbott & Costello, Fibber Magee and Molly, Lucy and Desi, Dean Martin and Jerry Lewis? Well, Bob Hope and Bing Crosby's partnership was not quite the same. Theirs was simply an informal marriage of two complex, diverse talents joined together for only special occasions. They didn't appear as a team except during the *Road* films, otherwise maintaining totally separate careers. Their offstage friendship was cordial, but never close. Most people assumed the personal side would be much like their association on the screen, but it was actually limited. Bing, an introvert on occasion, and Bob, always an extrovert, didn't hang out together. Under the camera or in front of the mike they had much fun working together, and audiences loved them. In all the *Road* films they meshed beautifully, but kept their professional identities separated from the personal.

Bob Hope attended every possible function, charitable or otherwise, and Bing simply avoided them. When an invited Bing failed to show up for a Friar's Club roast honoring Bob, Bob wondered why he didn't show up. Bing simply explained, "I wasn't hungry."

Bob, knowing Bing was an easy target for jokes because he was known to be wealthy (as was Bob), would say things like, "Instead of paying income tax, Bing just calls Washington and asks how much they need."

"My world collapsed when I had to hand Bing an Oscar for *Going My Way* when I emceed the Academy Awards in 1944. It was for the best acting performance of the year, knowing in my heart that I should have gotten it for smiling while I handed it to him."

*****

Bob Hope and Bing Crosby met for the first time at New York's Friars Club on 48th Street, the famous show business club that still exists at the same address. Several months later Bob introduced Bing to audiences on the great stage of the Capitol Theater in New York. Bing had just come off his first major feature film *The Big Broadcast of 1932*, after leaving Paul Whiteman's "King of Jazz" Orchestra, and striking out on his own. Bing's hit recording "I Surrender Dear" was riding high. The boys met afterwards at O'Reilly's Bar across from the Capitol and swapped stories, finding plenty to talk about in their respective careers. They even came up with a couple of routines while shooting billiards in the Friar's Club game room.

"We started to insult each other from the moment we met. I called him the sports shirt that walks like a man...and later...the large, economy size Sinatra. He called me 'The man with a nose like a bicycle seat."

BING: As I live, it's ski snoot.

BOB: Mattress hip.

BING: Shovel head.

BOB: Blubber.

BING: It's true. I met Bob Hope when I took an engagement at the Capitol Theater in New York. At that juncture, Hope and I hadn't begun to bully each other. That would come later.

"Lots of beefs with Robert. He coined the vulgarization 'groaner' for the word 'crooner.' The second time I saw him was at the Paramount. He had caught on and was doing pretty good. Someone came up with the idea of paring us in a picture called *The Road to Singapore*. As you now know, it worked out fine. Then we appeared on each other's radio shows. Our Hatfield-McCoy 'feud' just happened, it was not planned. The abusive dialogue was our kind of fun. Making films, we ad libbed like crazy, violating all the accepted rules. Our antics became accepted by the crew and even the director.

"About Hope and golf. We played for the Red Cross over a period stretching from 1941 to 1945 and we would hold a War Bond sale on the 18th green after the match. We auctioned off the balls, our clubs, golf apparel, and anything else we could find. The money always went for bonds. I lost count of the cities and courses we played on together."

The Road Pictures

Ted Crosby, Bing's brother and biographer

"A series of zany pictures were planned for Bing Crosby and Dorothy Lamour and a man who had been master of ceremonies at his show a few years before at the Capitol Theater in New York, a guy named Bob Hope. These three were to make, in succession, The Road to Singapore, The Road to Zanzibar, The Road to Morocco, and The Road to Utopia. Thus began the Bing Crosby-Bob Hope union, for here were two kindred souls whose common goal was to make people happy and have a good time doing it."

THE ROAD TO SINGAPORE (orig. Mandalay) — 1940
THE ROAD TO ZANZIBAR — 1941
THE ROAD TO MOROCCO — 1942
THE ROAD TO UTOPIA — 1946
THE ROAD TO RIO — 1948
THE ROAD TO BALI — 1953
THE ROAD TO HONG KONG — 1962

"BELIEVE IT OR NOT, HOPE HAS AN INTELLIGENT IDEA!"

says CROSBY

CROSBY:

Folks, this is fantastic, but old Hope has a great idea. He thinks *everybody* ought to give U.S. Savings Bonds for Christmas presents!

HOPE:

Thanks for the kind words, son. But no kidding, ladies and gentlemen, those Bonds are sensational. They're appropriate for *anyone* on your list. On Christmas morning, nothing looks better in a stocking—except maybe Dorothy Lamour.

CROSBY:

Old Ski Nose is correct. And don't forget how easy it is to buy bonds—you can get 'em at *any* bank or post office.

HOPE:

How about it, Mr. and Mrs. America? This Christmas let's *all* give U. S. Savings Bonds!

Give the Finest Gift of all...

U.S. SAVINGS BONDS

Legendary actor Anthony Quinn was very pleased to appear with Bob Hope and Bing Crosby in the infamous, vastly successful *Road* pictures. He was a *swarthy heavy* and always the ferocious antagonist:

"I was one of the few actors to be allied with Bing and Bob in those films. I became like a good-luck charm around the studio, because all the pictures that I was in at the time were making such enormous money; and of course, it was all due to Bing and Bob."

The first *Road* film was inaptly named *The Road to Mandalay*, but was changed to *The Road to Singapore* at the last minute. The premier was held in New York on April 13, 1940, forecasting instant success.

And, why not? Bob and Bing each had their own radio shows and appeared as guests on one another's programs. The formula? They simply stood on opposite sides of the microphone and threw insults at one another. Fans had listened to their shenanigans on the radio but, of course, had never seen them together. Their joint appearances in the "Road" films were a natural, for now the audiences could actually see them work their zany comedy together instead of just listening to them. The public adored Bob and Bing. Bing would stick close to the

Bing and Bob *(courtesy Paramount)*

SCENES
from

"THE ROAD TO
SINGAPORE"

·

A PARAMOUNT
PICTURE

The first Road picture
(courtesy Paramount)

lackadaisical, conversational formula which was his trademark.

The second film, the *Road to Zanzibar*, followed the same formula, including the continued presence of the lovely Dorothy Lamour. A former Miss New Orleans, Dorothy was another natural choice. She had appeared in South Sea Films in a sarong dress which Paramount admitted she looked great in and had developed quite a following of her own. As agreed among the Paramount executives, Bing would mostly get the girl. Even Bob and Bing's outrageous ad-libbing was an immense success:

Bob Hope and Bing Crosby in Road to Singapore

BING: "The two guys who developed the pictures for Paramount frowned on our ad libbing — fought like Hell against changing a word of their script. The stories were okay, but not really anything special. We didn't pay any attention to them and the writers would come on the set — and see us doing a scene that they had no recollection of writing. They would object, but we'd say, 'It's funny, it plays funny — what do you care?' So, they finally got inured to it and said 'Go ahead.'"

BOB HOPE: "We ad-libbed so much on the first couple of pictures that we almost got into trouble. On the radio we had the two top shows. People wanted to see us, because they understood our humor."

The truth is that Bob and Bing hired their own gag writer, Barney Dean, to step up the action in the otherwise limp script. Once, on the set, Bob bellowed, "If you hear one of your lines, yell Bingo!" One of the film's contracted writers got so mad, he left the set to file a complaint with Paramount executives.

Dorothy Lamour complained to the director and to the boys directly: "Please stop this nonsense. How am I going to say my lines? Just stop it!"

"You never knew what they were going to say. You kind of had the feeling that maybe they stayed home the night before and read their scripts to see who could outdo the other."

The *Road* films did not make sense. They just made money.

How many fans of the films remember the running gag, the famous "patty-cake" routine? That's when Bing and Bob were to initiate every fight, or prepare an exit, to the surprise of the bewildered antagonists.

The New York Times listed *Road to Utopia* as a better *Road* film. "Their style seems more refined, their timing a little more expert, their insults a little more acute." So with songs, dances, and a series of miraculous escapes, Bing Crosby and Bob Hope performed perfectly in all seven films, making them # 1 box office hits. They recorded eight songs together. The first two were "Put it There, Pal" and "Road to Morocco" from *Road to Morocco,*" "Chicago Style," "Hoot Man," and "The Merry Go Round," from *Road to Bali,* and from *The Road to Hong Kong*, "Team Work." "Nothing in Common" from *The Road to Hong Kong* and *Paris Holiday* were on the sound track of *Paris Holiday.*

The year 2000 commemorated the sixtieth anniversary of Bob and Bing's first Road film in 1940, *Road to Singapore.* Some consider those films to be of the most acclaimed comedy series in American film history.

"Bing and I never made the two more planned *Road* films, *Road to Moscow* and the *Road to the Fountain of Youth.* We were getting ready to shoot them when Bing got a casting call from Upstairs. He left us on a golf course in the middle of a swing."

When Bing passed away, Bob was stunned. The question of his own mortality, of course, surfaced. He canceled performances for a week, something he had never done before. Ward Grant, Bob's press agent, issued this note from Bob the following day:

"The whole world loved Bing with a devotion that not only crossed international boundaries but erased them. He made the world a single place through his music, spoke to it in a language that everybody understands — the language of the heart.

"No matter where you were in the world, because of Bing every Christmas was white, and because we had him with us — it'll always seem a little whiter.

"The world put Bing on a pedestal, but somehow I don't think he ever really knew it. Bing asked the world *Going My Way?* and we all were.

"Yesterday a heart may have stopped, and a voice stilled, but the real melody Bing sang will linger on as long as there is a phonograph to be played....and a heart to be lifted."

Bob was among the very few mourners permitted at the chapel of St. Paul the Apostle in Los Angeles when Bing Crosby was laid to rest in a hilltop grave.

*****

Note from the author:

As I'm writing this account of the *Road* films today, May 29, 2002, it is Bob Hope's birthday. He is 99 years old. Universal Studios, owner of the first four *Road* pictures, has reissued them on DVD (Direct Video Disc). Universal invited film and TV star Ann Jillian, television star Barbara Eden, comedienne Phyllis Diller and myself to narrate the infomercial heralding the film's re-release, commenting about Bob's and Bing's roles, as well as narrating the DVD features on the three additional Bob Hope films in the package. My 2002 book "The Spirit of Bob Hope" relates the story of the *Road* pictures from a *Hope* perspective.

Louis Armstrong

ARMSTRONG: "Bing had a voice that sounded like gold being poured out of a cup."

Bing and Louis have always been musically aligned.

Bing found inspiration in two bona fide trumpet players, Louis Armstrong and Bix Beiderbecke. Beiderbecke and Crosby were members of the Paul Whiteman Orchestra. Bing and Armstrong had been friends for many years.

"Just as Bix himself found inspiration in Armstrong out on the South side of Chicago in the late 1920s, so did I. Yes, I'm proud to acknowledge my debt to the Rev.Satchelmouth. He is the beginning and the end of music in America," Bing said in 1971.

Bing and Louis appeared together in the film *Pennies from Heaven* in 1936, which also starred the Jimmy Dorsey band. Jimmy had been a Whiteman alumni, too. It was Louis' first real movie break, thanks to Bing's influence. Louis was fea-

Bing and
Louis record-
ing, 1936
*(R. Grudens
collection)*

Bing and Louis in the recording studio
(R. Grudens collection)

tured in the "Skeleton in the Closet" sequence with a small group that included drummer Lionel Hampton. Bing and Louis also appeared and performed together in the 1938 film *Doctor Rhythm*. And then there was the polished and high-class film *High Society*, wherein Bing and Louis collaborated on Cole Porter's treasure "Now You Has Jazz," perhaps one of jazz's premier moments on film written expressly for the pair. In the film during that performance, Bing introduces Louis' musicians in the traditional one-by-one format preceding each players solo.

The Bing and Louis joyous collaboration of "Gone Fishin'" is another of their renowned recordings.

Decca's Jack Kapp first paired Bing and Louis in 1935, featuring them in every conceivable musical genre, a variety they never would have chosen themselves. Kapp, a prolific producer, understood the promotional angles and devised a way to keep both talents constantly aloft in the public eye.

The union of Louis and Bing reached back to the early days of Paul Whiteman when Bing and his friends sauntered uptown during their off hours to observe and listen to Louis and other pioneer jazz musicians at the famous Cotton Club. Later, when Bing was appearing on the West Coast at the Cocoanut Grove, he would hustle out after hours to the Cotton Club in Culver City to watch his pal Louis perform.

On Bing's radio show from 1949 through 1951, the two icons were paired on a number of different tunes like "A Kiss to Build a Dream On,' and "Lazy Bones." Audiences thoroughly enjoyed the collaborations of Louis Armstrong and Bing Crosby, and the two obviously enjoyed one another and spoke affectionately of each other, before, during, and after each performance.

Indeed, it was two totally different voices chanting one message; it was all beautiful music, within or without the jazz idiom.

The Andrews Sisters — Patty, Maxene & La Verne

My interviews with Patty Andrews 1982 - 2002

In the 1940s Bing Crosby and the Andrews Sisters trio were perfect singing partners in recorded music, managed by the ingenious Kapp Brothers at Decca Records.

Before that time, girl groups recorded mostly alone. There were The Brox Sisters, Dagmar and Lorraine, who were very popular in the first *Music Box Revue* in New York during the early twenties; The Dinning Sisters, Ginger, Lou, and Jean, who performed on *National Barn Dance*, an NBC regular radio show; the Barry Sisters, Claire and Merna, who sang mostly ethnic music in a variety of venues; and the very popular Boswell Sisters, Connee, Martha, and Vet, who were the first national favorites to sing with Bing. But it was the three Andrews Sisters, Patty, Maxene, and La Verne, from Minneapolis who garnered the most commercial success and performed regularly with Bing, thanks to the vision of Decca Records President Jack Kapp. According to Bing and the girls, the four performers had plenty of fun.

The Andrews Sisters were defined as the best female voices of their era and recognized as the definitive female voices of

Patty, Maxene, and LaVerne sing to Bing in *Road to Rio*, 1948

World War II. They worked regularly with the creme-de-la-creme of orchestras: the Dorseys, Les Brown, Guy Lombardo, Fred Waring, Woody Herman, Buddy Rich, Joe Venuti, Xavier Cugat, Glenn Miller, and even Benny Goodman. But it was their recordings with Bing Crosby, who was then Decca's biggest star, that placed them on national charts.

"We sure was nervous about singing with a big star like Bing. I couldn't look him in the eye, I was so edgy. For the moment I didn't think I could sing. He had a funny way of moving his foot around like a metronome, and it calmed me. Bing was so nice to me and my sisters. He made me feel comfortable because he knew of my apprehension. He called me 'Pat,' and would sometimes hold my hand which made me feel better.

"We recorded lots of great sides together like 'South American Way,' Ciribiribin,' 'Yodelin' Jive (which became an early top ten hit), 'Pistol Packin' Mama,' 'The Victory Polka,' 'Jingle Bells,' 'Don't Fence Me In,' 'Apalachicola, F-L-A,' You Don't Have to Know the Language,' and the Hawaiian Christmas song 'Mele Kalikimaka' and even more.

"We loved working with Bing," Patty continued. "It was always so exciting. He always would do something unexpected, like the time he sneaked in that line at the end of 'Pistol Packin' Momma' — 'Lay that thing down before it goes off and hurts someone.' And Bing would always want to record at eight in the morning," she revealed. "I guess he used to vocalize in the car on the way to the studio — and he always wore his golf clothes. He always claimed his voice had a husky quality in the morning."

It was said that Bing would always settle for a final on the first take. According to Patty, "I secretly believe he did it that way so he could get out on the golf course earlier."

Long before the sisters became professional singers, they would listen to Bing and the Boswell Sisters on his early radio programs, and were entranced by them. "We would copy the Boswell's style and even tried to imitate their Southern drawl," Patty smiled as she recalled, "But we gave up the drawl. We were just three Greek girls from Minneapolis, Minnesota."

The Andrews' three part harmony mastery began for them at a very early age. Patty was about seven and performed the lead, which lasted throughout their careers. Maxine sang second part harmony with a more soprano sound, and LaVerne handled the third part, contralto and bass.

It is safe to say that Bing Crosby and the Andrews Sisters were indeed the top 1940s stars of the recording industry. The girls also traveled and entertained with Bing, Bob Hope, and Dorothy Lamour selling World War II War Bonds, and appeared with the trio in the movie *Road to Rio*.

"Bing Crosby was one of the most important people in our lives and we loved him. We really did. I think of him often," Patty reminisces. "We were very lucky."

Rhonda Fleming

My interview in September 2002.

In late August of 2002 I talked with beautiful Rhonda Fleming about her friend and fellow actor Bing Crosby. Rhonda and I have worked together on recent books I wrote about her good friend, singer Connie Haines, and Bob Hope, with whom she made some films. Here's what she had to say:

....
"A Connecticut Yankee in King Arthur's Court", with Rhonda Fleming (courtesy Paramount)
....

"Through the years I've been asked many times, 'Which of your forty films were your favorites?' I always responded with 'What made a film memorable and special to me were the stars and actors I worked with, and my number one favorite was Bing Crosby in *A Connecticut Yankee in King Arthur's Court.* He was delightful, funny, charming, and treated me (a new-comer), like a queen — making sure the hair, the costume, the make-up was just right for my very first Technicolor film and insisting I co-star above the title with him since he never want-ed his name alone. Can you believe — my very first starring role and billing above the title, no less — thanks to Bing, it was like a fairy tale!

"Of all my favorites, he was the most natural actor I ever worked with and one of the most deliciously charming men I've encountered. He was at his very best in that film and it's become a classic all over the world.

"Bing was always telling jokes on the set to make people laugh. We'd be ready to shoot a scene and I was ready to go like a race horse at the gate and Bing would be talking to the men up on the catwalks. He'd be telling them a funny story...and while trying to remember my lines and listening to the joke, the director would shout 'action.' Bing would go immediately from the joke right into his scene. He didn't for-get a word or a movement. The minute the director said 'cut,' Bing was back to finishing the joke again. What an incredible memory!"

Jack Benny

From his daughter's book *Sunday Nights at Seven*

JACK: To appreciate this story you have to realize that in those days there was no such thing as taping radio shows in advance — it was all *live*. During a spot on Jack Benny's show where Bing sang in a quartet with Dick Haymes, Andy Russell and Dennis (Day), Bing had to sing a note that was much higher than his normal baritone range. Instead of the usual Crosby sound, he sang a hideous squeal. This upset him and when his voice creaked on the high note, he forgot about the quartet and snarled, "Who in the hell picked this key — Dennis Day?

"Well, you must remember that in 1947 you did not say words like 'hell,' 'damn,' 'bastard,' or 'pregnant' on the air.

Secondly, in several recent pictures, most notably in the Academy Award winner, *Going My Way*, Bing had been playing a Catholic priest.

"As soon as Bing said the magic word "hell, all *heck* broke loose on every member station of the NBC network and all the switchboards lit up and thousands of irate listeners called to register their shock at "Father" Crosby's blasphemy.

"After the show, an NBC vice president was waiting for me in the dressing room. He was fretting and fuming. He was sure the writers wrote that line. It wasn't in the submitted script so it couldn't be censored. I told him it was *just* — "*Bing.*" He didn't believe me.

"He blamed me for the whole thing. 'An awful thing,' he repeated over and over: 'You'll have to apologize. Your writers have to issue a statement justifying things. The sponsor, Lucky Strike Cigarettes, will have to apologize.'

"I waited until he finished blowing off steam. Finally, he was out of breath.

"You listen to me, I said. *Nobody* is going to apologize.

"He started to scream again.

"I raised my hand to silence him: 'The *only* thing that is going to happen is that in Bing's next movie, he will wear his collar frontwards, and *that's* all.'

"He didn't think that was very funny.

"Bing did.

"And I did."

Bing carries Jack Benny to his vault, 1945
(R. Grudens collection)

James Cagney

"During the war, at our opening show at Soldier Field, Chicago, there was a crowd of 130,000. Bing walked out to a reception for which the adjective 'triumphant' is inadequate. He stood there in that very humble, charming way of his. After the audience explosion died down, Bing said, 'Whadda yez wanna hear?' and they exploded again until the stadium walls nearly buckled. After they subsided, he said, 'Ya wanna leave it to me?' and they blew up again. Finally, he said, 'Hit me, Al,' to our orchestra leader Al Newman, who started his boys off on 'Blues in the Night.' They had played only the first two bars when the audience went into rapturous applause once more. Bing finished the song, and never in my life have I heard anything like it. I got the traditional goose pimples just standing there, listening. He did another, same thing. When Bing came offstage, the perspiration on him was an absolute revelation to me. Here he had been to all appearances perfectly loose and relaxed, but not at all. He was giving everything he had in every note he sang, and the apparent effortlessness was a part of his very hard work."

Bing always stated that his appearance at that show was his greatest moment in show business.

Bing, Hedy Lamarr, James Cagney and Kay Kyser broadcast to the troops duing the war
(R. Grudens collection)

Peggy Lee

Drawn from my 1982 interview with Peggy

"Before I met Bing, I had always secretly loved the Rodgers and Hart song 'Down By the River' that he sang years before in the 1935 film *Mississippi*, and I told him how I felt about it. One night, when I went to dinner with him at a little place in

San Francisco, he actually sang it for me. He somehow convinced the piano player to play it and then sang it to me personally. Can you imagine that? It was a memorable evening. There was always a certain security for me in just thinking of Bing. He was always finding ways to help give me confidence. "In fact, everyone connected with him was funny and nice and talented.

"Bing and I were always the first to arrive for rehearsals. I was always impressed by his promptness, his honesty and modesty. It amazed me that he was so humble. I tried to tell him the world thought so highly of him, but I don't think I ever convinced him.

Peggy Lee
(courtesy Peggy Lee)

"He was always so protective and so sensitive during my early days of nerves and self-consciousness. Just before air time on one of my first Kraft programs, he found me standing rigid outside the studio at NBC and asked me what he could do to help. I managed to say, 'When you introduce me, would you please not leave me out there on the stage alone? Would you stand where I can see your feet?'

Tony Bennett

"From then on he always casually leaned against a speaker or piano to give me the support I needed to learn about being at ease on stage. And he offered everything — money -cars, his own blood, and even volunteered to baby sit with our little daughter, Nicki, while my husband, Dave Barbour, was so sick in the hospital.

"You have to love a man like that."

Tony Bennett

Drawn from my 1984 and 1988 interviews with Tony.

"Bing loved to sing — you could hear it in every recording. He wasn't concerned with making hit recordings or insuring a particular song a success, he simply loved to sing. And could he sing! He sang with just about everyone in the business, fellow singer or almost every known band of his time. There were no ego problems so he got along well with his fellow performers. My Uncle Dick told me once in a very serious voice, 'There is one singer who has changed the face of this music business. You must watch everything he does. His name is Bing Crosby and he's the boss.'

"From that day on, I studied Bing. He is the one who has shown us all how to do it. He developed a relaxing attitude and style which appealed to everybody...a style that got under your skin. This was a revelation for singers, and Bing was the most popular singer of all time. Bigger than Elvis and the Beatles combined."

Rosemary Clooney

Drawn from my 1986 interview with Rosemary.

In the enjoyable motion picture *White Christmas*, a film crowded with spirited Irving Berlin tunes that still evoke tears and raises goose bumps for its sentimentality, Rosemary Clooney plays Bing's love interest. Rosemary joyfully finds herself singing duets with her hero Bing Crosby. "Love You Didn't Do Right by Me" and "Count Your Blessings" are executed beautifully, perhaps showcasing her

Bing and Rosie, "Count your Blessings," (courtesy Paramount)

best singing performances on film. She took much delight vocalizing with Bing, whom she considered her musical mentor, personal promoter, and true friend. The film also starred prolific comedian/dancer Danny Kaye and dancer Vera-Ellen.

ROSEMARY: "Bing and I were very good friends, but neither of us could read music. Everyone is surprised to learn that fact about us. We were always comfortable with each other and used our own separate performance systems when we sang duets. And we did just that on radio, television, and in movies. We blended beautifully, because Bing allowed it. This film was strictly Bing's. He chose the cast, approved the director and in a quiet way, oversaw the production. He picked me. He wanted Fred Astaire, but Fred was busy with another project. Then he tried to get Donald O'Connor, but he became ill. One day, Sylvia Fine, Danny Kaye's wife, asked me to talk to Bing about him doing the picture. Of course, Danny did the film beautifully."

After Dixie Lee's passing Bing would bring his kids to Rosemary's house in Beverly Hills.

ROSEMARY: "They would stand outside and sing carols, then they would come in for some hot chocolate and we'd slip them a few bucks. Little Lindsay once said to his Dad, 'Hey, Dad, we should come here all the time. Uncle Everett only gives us a dime.'

"When I had my son Miguel, Bing was recovering from a kidney stone operation in the same hospital. His nurse was informed by my nurse that I had a boy, and Bing was happy he learned about it first, even before my husband, actor Jose Ferrer. Joe really admired Bing, but, for some reason, was always a little nervous around him."

JOSE' FERRER: "Al Jolson was like Mr. Great Singer of all time. Maurice Chevalier was like Mr. Entertainer of all time. Frank Sinatra is like Mr. Balladeer of all time. But Bing Crosby is like Mr. Everything of all time."

ROSEMARY: "I found that the best way to get along with Bing was to forget that he was *Bing Crosby*, that is, if you could. Every once in a while I would realize the reality and would say to myself,'What the hell am I doing singing here with *Bing Crosby*?

"To me, Bing retained a tremendous personal dignity and reserve that was not easy to penetrate. When he finally decided to make personal appearances, something he didn't do throughout most of his career except at USO shows during World War II, I saw in his face when he was taking a bow at the end of a show — his attitude towards the audience and their outpouring of love for him. Everyone on their feet roaring their approval visibly moved him. This happened just a few years before he passed on."

When Rosemary and Kathryn Crosby visited Buckingham Palace before Rosemary and Bing performed at the Palladium, they were chatting, then suddenly noticed that the Queen had unexpectedly walked into the room:

ROSEMARY: "I had a sherry in one hand and my purse in the other, and realized I'd have to get rid of the sherry very quickly because she was approaching us and I had to have a hand free. I flipped the glass on a passing footman's tray and greeted the Queen who stopped and talked to Kathryn and I for about twenty minutes."

They talked about families and children. Here were three ladies, Kathryn, Rosemary, and the Queen — the wife of a legend, an Irish American singer, and a reigning monarch — who stripped away positions and politics to discuss what any other three woman anywhere else in the world would have discussed.

ROSEMARY: "I thought we were really all quite basic.

"Bing cared, but was the kind of a man who would never intrude on what he felt was something private. He was a gentleman and I'm privileged to have had him as a trusted friend and have had so many wonderful times and shared many memories with him over the years."

Bing Crosby and Rosemary Clooney shared many duets together on their CBS radio shows from 1952 through 1954, on The Ford CBS radio shows throughout 1958, Bing's CBS radio show from 1960 through 1962, and on dozens of recorded duets on television through March of 1977.

Author's Note: Sadly, as I complete writing these words on a Sunday morning, June 30, 2002, news of Rosemary Clooney's sudden passing abruptly closes this otherwise beautiful tribute to Bing.

Les Paul

From My interview with Les Paul in 1998

Les Paul, legendary guitarist and pioneer multi-track recording inventor, known to all as the Wizard of Waukesha, began his career playing on WRJN radio in Racine, Wisconsin, with his Sears & Roebuck mail order guitar and Hohner harmonica when he was a fledgling 10 year old musician, and about twenty-one when he formed the Les Paul Trio. Bing Crosby's personal guitarist, Eddie Lang, was his idol:

"I would get some Paul Whiteman King of Jazz Orchestra records and listen to Eddie backing Bing, and playing with [jazz violinist] Joe Venuti. That's when I decided to get serious. Eddie could play all the great stuff, harmonics, hammering on, pulling strings,and great vibrato, too. When I had just formed the Les Paul Trio, we knew Bing Crosby was at the height of

....
"How High
the Moon?"
Les Paul
and Mary
Ford in 1952
*(courtesy
Downbeat
Magazine)*
....

his fame as a crooner, so I arranged for the trio to rehearse in an NBC studio adjacent to Crosby's."

They were heavily into "Back Home in Indiana," when Bing opens the door:

"Oh! I'm sorry, I didn't know there was anybody in here."

"That's okay. Come on in."

Bing walked in and proceeded to the piano. Leaning against it, he said, "Wait a minute, what's the name of this outfit?"

"The Les Paul Trio."

"Where do you work?"

"Right here at NBC."

"M-m-m. Well you don't work here anymore."

"We don't?"

"No," smiled Bing,"You work for me. I just hired you."

Bing started to leave.

"Hey, Bing, how much are you paying me?"

"A thousand dollars."

"Hey, Bing, how much for the other two guys?"

The trio and Bing cut their first record, "It's Been A Long, Long, Time," a big Decca hit in that prolific Bing Crosby year of 1945. The two icons enjoyed working together for many years hence. Les toured with Bing and the Andrews Sisters. At one time Bing offered Les Paul the backing to set up a private studio and music school, but Les turned him down, and instead set up a studio in a detached garage at his home in West Hollywood where he conducted early experiments in developing multitracking with homemade equipment . Throughout his life, Les Paul had fulfilled opportunities by wrangling attachments to artists like Bing Crosby and seizing the moment like that extraordinary setup to snare Crosby in that NBC studio.

"It's ironic," Les Paul told me at his mountainside home in Mahwah, New Jersey, just a few seasons ago, "I took Eddie's place backing Bing Crosby. It's where I always wanted to be."

Fred Astaire

From his autobiography.

"In *Holiday Inn*, Bing Crosby and I worked very hard together. Bing was easy to dance with. He used to joke about

Top: Fred Astaire
(R. Grudens collection)
Bottom: With Fred
Astaire in France during
a 1944 USO Tour
(courtesty USO)

it. He's certainly not a dancer. I call him the kind of dancer that I am a singer.

"But he works hard and we had a few steps designed so that we could work them together. When later people asked me who was my favorite dancing partner, I would always say Bing Crosby. It cleared me from having to name one of my lady partners."

Mel Tormé

**My interview with Mel in 1985
and memoirs from his two books.**

"One New Year's Eve Day, we were invited to lunch at Bing Crosby's, just outside of San Francisco. Earlier, a disc jockey from Boston played a tape for me on the phone. To my amazement, the tape was his interview with Bing."

D.J.: "Bing, if you got stuck on a desert island with nothing more than a phonograph and a few records, whose records would you most want to have?"

BING: "Well, of course, some of the great jazz players — Teagarden and, oh, you know, guys like that that. Oh, and Mel Tormé's records ....I tell you, any singer that goes in to hear this guy sing has got to go out and cut his throat. He's the most fantastic musical performer I think we've ever had...the best musical entertainer I've ever seen."

Mel Tormé
(R. Grudens collection)

"To me, Bing's remarks were amazing. I wrote him thanks and wondered if he would mind if I used some of what he said in my publicity stuff. He wrote back saying okay, but added more plaudits in his letter, which he said I may use, too. He had come to see me at the Fairmont Hotel the previous year. Now, here's the greatest popular singer of our century praising my work — that was mind-blowing.

"On New Year's Eve Day, 1975, my wife Jan; Bing's kids, Harry, Mary Frances, and

Nathaniel, and Kathryn; Bing; and myself were having a funny, happy and gabby meal in Bing's dining room. Then, Bing leads us into his music room. There was the great one without his toupee' — no pretense, mind you. He tells little Harry to get his guitar. Harry strums a popular James Taylor tune and Bing joins in and sings... singing for us, mind you. Incredible!

"Then Bing asks *me* to sing and I go to the piano and play my new song 'Christmas was Made for Children.' I give him a copy. He likes it. Wonderful!

"When we left Bing tells me the whole family is going to come to the Fairmont to see me. I couldn't believe it. Bing smiles and says, 'I'll see you later.'

"He shows up with the whole family as promised. What a night. Bing Crosby thinks I'm a great performer. His whole family responded so beautifully. Kathryn was wonderful and supporting.

"You know, a book was written about Bing, painting him as a cold, thoughtless man. No way! Every encounter with Bing was memorable, warm, and filled with great, good humor. He always treated me, and others I know, as equals — a perfect person. How good could it get."

Bing Crosby and Mel Tormé recorded two songs together: "Day by Day" and "Prove It By the Things You Do."

Mary Martin

Broadway Star

"After making the movie *Victor Herbert*, I made *Rhythm on the River* with Bing. We were fooling around on the set one day and Harry Barris was doodling 'Shoe Shine Boy' on the piano. Bing walked over and said, 'I used to hear a girl sing that in a nightclub. I went there every night to hear her. Then she disappeared and I lost track of her.'

"I walked straight over to Bing and said, 'You like that song? Sit down and I'll sing it for you.' I still knew my old arrangement. All the time I sang he stared, his eyes becoming wider and his smile wider.

"When I finished, he said, 'That's the way that girl sang it.'
'Well, Bing Crosby,' I told him, 'I'm that girl.'
"He couldn't believe it.

"Maybe if Bing had 'discovered' me two years before, my break would have come sooner. I doubt it, though, because I wasn't ready yet. Bing and I still have 'Shoe Shine Boy' as a bond, and I still love that song. It makes a great lullaby for grandchildren.

"Making movies with Bing almost made Hollywood worthwhile. He is the most relaxed, comfortable, comforting man. No matter what happens he can ad-lib, cover up, carry on. He can even sing with gum in his mouth, he just parks it over on one side. While we were making films we also sang together on the *Kraft Music Hall* on radio. I've seen him a hundred times drop his entire script in midshow and go right on singing. He'd just lean over, grope around with his hand to find the script, pick it up, and find his place instantly. He never missed a note.

"Every time I looked at him I thought to myself again, "Be careful what you wish, it might come true." For years now I've said it to my friends. Back in my popcorn eating Palace Theater days in Weatherford, I wished and wished and wished that some day I could meet and work with my three dream men — Bing Crosby, Maurice Chevalier, and Noel Coward. Well, I did it!"

Jack Ellsworth

New York Radio WALK, From my interview in 2002

Jack Ellsworth of New York radio WALK, Long Island, has a daily show he named *Memories in Melody*. Jack celebrated his 80th birthday in late June, 2002. His program had been on the air continually for over 51 years, and everyday, on every show, he opens with a Count Basie, followed by Nat "King" Cole, an Ella Fitzgerald, then selections from Glenn Miller's "live" broadcasts emanating from either the Glen Island Casino, the *Chesterfield Show*, or the Cafe Rouge in New

York's Hotel Pennsylvania, as well as several daily selections of young Bing Crosby. The Crosby selections are not always Bing's most popular recordings. Jack, who has a great following and an even greater music library, treats his listeners with many Crosby rare recordings, as well as recordings from many other performers like Jerry Vale, Frank Sinatra, and Perry Como. Jack still airs the longest running Sinatra radio show that has also been on the air over fifty years, and it has been personally acknowledged by Sinatra himself by way of exclusive recorded promos.

Jack knew Bing and interviewed him a year before his death. Here is a portion of that interview:

JACK: "Bing, in the thirties and forties, young people had a greater opportunity to break into show business through an association with the bands...like you did with Paul Whiteman and Frank did it with Tommy Dorsey. What can a young person do today, someone who feels they have talent and wants to move ahead? What direction would they take today?"

BING: "Well, Jack, in my time there wasn't much competition, when you consider that the only people singing the way I sang would be Rudy Vallee, Ozzie Nelson, Russ Columbo...only five or six fellows. Will Osborne was another...so there really wasn't too much competition. Now, the competition is fierce. I think if someone has talent they should give it a whirl....sing as often as they can...any place, schools, parish entertainment, wherever they can get up on their feet and sing.

L to R. Jack Ellsworth plays Bing everyday on "Memories in Melody" while band-leader Ben Grisafi approves

"Sing around the house, like I did, and learn poise and presence and ease and just take a good whack at it. If it does-n't come off, drop it quickly. Don't get hooked on something that's going to be futile. You'll be better off. Drop it and get into a different, more worthwhile activity if you find you can't make it professionally. But, on the other hand, if you believe you can do it, be sure to give it a try. Let somebody tell you whether or not you have real talent for advancement, and whether you have a good feel for tempo, rhythm or for timing and reading lines, or whatever. Let some expert take a listen at you and give you an idea. And, don't be discouraged if he tells you he doesn't think you can do it...you gave it a real try. Just drop it and get into something else."

Phil Harris
Bandleader, comedian

"A lot of people don't understand Bing because he goes his own way, minds his own business, picks his own friends and lives on his own. I first met Bing in 1927 when he and Al Rinker were doing a one-nighter and I was a drummer in the band, and we moved on as friends. We did a lot of hunting and fishing together. We'd hang out together and he was always singing or whistling something or the other. Bing also had a great memory for faces. He really was a guy who enjoyed relaxing.

"If I didn't see him from time to time, 'cause I led the band on Jack Benny's radio show and we didn't see each other often, but we would still get together, and sometimes my wife Alice (Faye) would come along, but the girls usually stayed home. Since Bing passed over, I never went hunting or fishing again. So I still miss him. Bing had more friends than you could count. I was proud to one of his best friends."

There's a great story Bing told about Phil Harris, a man who liked his Jack Daniels whisky. Phil could make Bing laugh until he had a stomach ache and had to leave the room:

"It was about midnight and we were driving downtown Los Angeles near where they had a big distillery. It's midnight and the distillery is going full blast, steam pouring out of the chimneys, all the lights burning. So, I said, 'You see Phil, no matter how much you drink, they're going to keep ahead of you.' Yeah,' he said, 'But I've got 'em working nights, haven't I?'"

Herbert Mills

The Mills Brothers

"We were working the Paramount Theater in New York, all on the same bill. There was Bing, Kate Smith — a slew of

The Mills
Brothers. L
to R: Herb,
Harry and
Donald, 1960
(Mills Brothers
Society)

people on the stage together. We were thirteen weeks with the show, then went on to the Paramount in Brooklyn — the whole bunch. Russ Columbo joined us there. The Mills Brothers made about four recordings including the 1928 version of 'Tiger Rag,' before doing one with Bing. We had a lot of fun. Bing and my brother Donald, the youngest Mills, were able to 'scat sing'. It went just wonderful. When Bing had his radio show, we were on with him for eight months till he wrapped it up. He went on the road and we went to the California Cotton Club. Bing was always great to work with — he was a natural."

"My Honey's Lovin' Arms" is a great Mills Brothers Bing Crosby recording.

Joe Franklin

My interview with Joe and his with Bing.

In late August of 2002, Joe Franklin recalled for me his fascinating interview with Bing Crosby in 1976, which has become a classic. Joe had joined up with WOR radio back in

1967, where he originated his long running show *Down Memory Lane*, then moved into television. His show has become the benchmark of all interview shows. It is still on the air. Joe said the Crosby interview is his all-time favorite of the thousands of interviews he has conducted over the years on radio and television. For him it was the flesh and blood meeting with Bing that punctuated his career as being the highlight of all he has accomplished as a host for over 50 years. Joe generously shares the interview with Bing and Kathryn:

BING: (The studio crew welcomes Bing with enthusiastic applause.) That's a nice reception and I'm always glad to be in this environment with all these hard working folks, and my friend Joe here.

JOE: Bing, my hero, my favorite entertainer of all time, let's talk about things happening to you today...right now.

BING: First, Joe, let's talk about Kathryn and I performing at the Uris Theater here in New York where we open December 7th and play through the 19th. We have a little act we've been doing since last summer all over the country and in Europe, and all for charity. It includes Rosie Clooney and Kathryn and our children, as well as Joe Bushkin's quartet, and an English comic Ted Rogers, and I bark a few ditties in and out — I groan a few, yeah, but we don't make a penny. And thanks to Joe for this substantial plug. So come on over folks. Help your local charities. All the proceeds go to help retarded children in this case.

JOE: I already bought my tickets. Say, Bing, one of my production men, Randolph, who used to work with you at the New York Paramount, told me you never had to warm up like other singers before a performance, you know, like going up and down the scale. You would just walk out cold, you didn't have to gargle or warm up your pipes.

BING: True, true. Nothing would help me. I just took my best shot and prayed that it would work. Sometimes it did and sometimes it didn't. Randolph worked with me for a number of years and he knows.

JOE: Bing, weren't you involved in producing television shows with Crosby Television Productions?

BING: Sure, we produce some nice things including *Ben Casey*, our biggest, and *Hogan's Heroes* — both Crosby Productions, and not doing bad I might say. *Hogan's* goes on and and on and on. But, it's a tough business, you know, producing for television. So many pilots are made but only a few get through. And sometimes they are great but they are up against some tough competition that kills them in the ratings, and they never get a shot even though they may be great. A bloody battle, for sure.

JOE: Bing, I've heard three versions of how Harry Lillis became *Bing*...tell us how it really happened.

BING: Sure, I'll give you the authentic version. When I was a kid three or four years old, there was a comic strip called the *Bingville Bugle* with a character in it named Bingo, something like the comics "Katzenjammer Kids" or "Happy Hooligan," and a neighbor, a kid a few years older than me with the name of — (pause) Valentine Hobart, he called me *Bingo*, then it was cut short to Bing. But, my mother always called me Harry. That's the true and only.

JOE: Bing, how about you introducing your lovely wife Kathryn to the audience.

BING: Oh, this is a little girl from West Columbia, Texas, who came to the Paramount studio where I was working, and she was under contract then, and she was writing a column for a little paper in Texas about her impressions of Hollywood and the people she met. She came by my dressing room. I saw her walking by, a very prim, little Texas girl, bouncing along, and I said, "Hi, Tex," and she stopped and we had tea and that started a friendship that developed into a romance and finally led to the altar.

KATHRYN: (Mischievously) Wouldn't *you* have stopped? There's nobody in the world who wouldn't have dropped their petticoat (Bing raises his brow and shakes his head).

JOE: Kathryn, what makes the world nicer or better for you with Bing in it?

KATHRYN: The overwhelming thing is music, Joe: ease and nice and fun, and... music! Somebody asked, "Isn't there...are there, hardships involved with being Mrs. Bing Crosby?" And, I thought, yeah... if you don't like music or lovely friends that are warm and friendly to you, then it's very tough. But, if you like music or like people who are fond of your husband, and nothing can be more flattering, it's terribly pleasing to me, Joe, (She turns to face Bing sitting to her left) — Don't blush darling — (Bing groans), almost any woman...I've not met one woman in the world that would'nt be delighted to change places with me.

BING: No... get outta here.....!

JOE: Who would have the final say if there is any difference of opinion at home? Bing, you would have it?

BING: I don't think it ever resolved any difference of opinion. Kathryn is firm, she sticks with her belief and I stick with mine and we just stop talking about it and let it go away and finally it dissolves and we forget about it.

KATHRYN: That's a great thing Bing has taught me, Joe. I was brought up to believe that difficulties must be faced and solved, and there are an awful lot of things in life that can't be solved, and really don't have to be faced, unless you are a masochist and like to look at unhappy things and sometimes you just let things fly. You go fishing!

BING: You talk about it as long as you can and then if it seems insolvable, then the only thing is to go fishing or go golfing and then the seriousness will abate and you are finished with it.

KATHRYN: That's true. Things always get easier after awhile. Time heals.

JOE: Kathryn, how can Bing be so modest? Will you help read something to the audience? Somebody asked Bing the secret of his great success, and Bing, you have to tell me if you actually said this to a newspaper man who wrote this.

BING: All right.

KATHRYN: (Reading from a book handed to her by Joe Franklin) Every man who sees one of my movies or who listens to my records or who hears me on the radio believes firmly that he sings as well as I do, especially when he's in the bathroom shower. It's no trick for him to believe this because I have none of the mannerisms of a trained singer and I have very little voice.

JOE: Now Bing...you really said that once?

BING: I did. I still think that it's true. I think that if I have any appeal, that's the reason for it. I don't think I have any right to be to put on any sides...I don't think I'm that good. .....or be pompous. I think a lot of fellers sing great...I've heard them.

BING: Joe hands Bing an album of Bing related songs Bing then sings a few bars *a cappella* of each selection listed on the record jacket: He sings the first line or so of each song: "Ramona," "If I Had You," "Call Me Darling," "Out of Nowhere," "April Showers," "Where the Blue of the Night Meets the Gold of the Day..." Hey, how did this get in here? "A good man is Hard to Find," "Just One More Chance," "I Found a Million Dollar Baby in a Five and Ten Cents Store," Now, this is Russ' (Columbo) song, "You Call it Madness — I Call it Love,") — I don't remember the rest of the song.

JOE: Hey, crew, and Arthur Tracy, (the famous Street Singer) who has just joined us, how about this homemade medley. (The television studio crew, encouraged by Joe Franklin, applauds long and loudly)

ARTHUR TRACY: And, Bing, you haven't changed.

JOE: Bing, we have to listen to my favorite Crosby record, I know it's corny or smaltzy, but I have to play it. Bing, if you want to say a few words about "White Christmas," or to Mr. Irving Berlin, who is watching this, go right ahead.

BING: Is Mr. Irving Berlin listening? Irving, how nice to talk to you. I put out a new album in England lately and one of your songs is in it and I think you would like to hear it. I'm gonna send you a copy. It's called "When I Leave the World Behind" — you remember that! And "White Christmas," of course, you know what it's done for me and how grateful I am to you. It made my career you know, really, musically. Anybody who gets a stimulus like that directly attributed to you, has to be eternally grateful, and I am.

JOE: Kathryn, when you look at Bing, it's so beautiful...how you look into his eyes...she's almost crying the way you're talking to Irving Berlin. (Bing singing "White Christmas" is playing in the background)

JOE: Just a taste of the biggest selling record ever made "White Christmas."

JOE: Bing has to go, but before they go I want Kathryn to tell us why she fell in love with Bing Crosby, and, it was not his singing voice. It was...(pointing to Kathryn).

KATHRYN: ...his speaking voice! You were the one who picked it up, Joe. Its the quality of his speaking that draws you in. It's impossible to be angry with him when he says, now-w, Kathryn.

Words from Connie Haines, Jerry Vale, Frankie Laine, and hostess Sally Bennett.

Connie Haines

Connie Haines, who sang with Frank Sinatra in the Harry James and Tommy Dorsey bands of the forties and toured for five years with the Abbott & Costello traveling radio show, often appeared with Bing on his radio show with guests like Phil Silvers, Betty Grable, and other great stars.

"On one particular *Command Performances* show during World War II, a radio transcription that was broadcast to our soldiers overseas, the script called for Bing, Bob Hope, and Frank Sinatra to be bickering over who was to take me to dinner after the show. I don't know who was funnier, Bing, with his quick wit, or Bob with his very funny ad libs. Of course, in reality, we all went to dinner together after the show and

Phil Silvers,
Bing, Betty
Grable and
Connie
Haines
*(Connie Haines
collection)*

enjoyed a great time and had more laughs than you could believe. It was truly a memorable show. And what a time to be in show business and being able to work alongside the unforgettable talents of someone like Bing Crosby.

"Once, when Jane Russell, Beryl Davis and I were in the Decca recording studios recording 'Do Lord.' I can't tell you how many takes it took. We almost gave up, instead we all said a prayer and tried again. We had lost count of the takes when...someone shouted, 'That's it!' It was Bing, who had stopped in to listen. 'You gals have a hit...maybe a million seller. How about that.' Bing said with much enthusiasm. Just to have seen Bing would have shaken us up, but to have him walk in and say we have a million seller on our hands was one of the thrills of our lives, something we still talk about today. Bing was right on target with his prediction. It became the most

Bing Crosby
—Hollywood—

September 17, 1963

Dear Mrs. Bennett:

Mrs. Crosby handed me your material
when I was in Warren last week.

It seems like good material, but quite
honestly, my recording is limited these
days to standards, and I would not have
use for it.

You might try some of the new group -

Yours,

Bing Crosby

BC:lm

Enclosures

Mrs. Paul Bennett
19859 Beach Cliff Boulevard
Rocky River, Ohio

....
Letter from Bing to Sally
....

important singing success of our lives."

Jerry Vale

Jerry Vale emulated the voices of Bing Crosby, Perry Como and Frank Sinatra, the three most popular singers of his time. "Growing up in the Bronx, I listened to *The Battle of the Baritones* radio show on station WINS and tried very hard to sing like Bing, hoping for a future for myself singing the same kind of songs. I sang for hours, absorbing every phrase, every rest, memorizing every style, and held notes for as long as I could. That self-training device worked for me, so I have to acknowledge my thanks to Bing, Frank, and Perry, who taught me all I know about the business of singing."

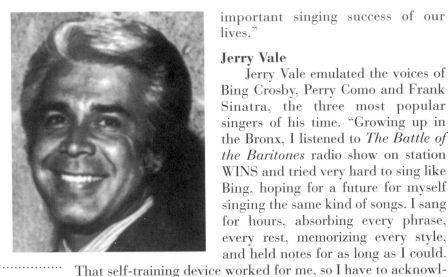

Jerry Vale
(R. Grudens collection)

Frankie Laine

Frankie Laine emulated Bing during Marathon Days singing "Straight from the Shoulder."

Bing with
Frankie Laine
(R. Grudens collection)

"Of course, Bing was the champ in those days and everybody wanted to hear Bing or Bing style singers. Russ Columbo, Perry Como, and a budding Frank Sinatra all tried to sound like Bing. When asked to sing during the dance marathon craze, I would sing mainly Bing tunes like 'I Surrender, Dear' because crooning was a brand new thing and I was just knocked out by Bing's sound. I used to imitate him so closely that people said I sounded more like Bing and he

did himself." When Perry Como sang with Ted Weems, he was just another up and coming Bing sounding crooner. Frankie Laine appeared on Bing's show *Philco Radio Time* on November 26, 1947, worth noting for the opportunity it provided Frank to exchange quips with its genial host, and his singing idol, Bing Crosby.

Sally Bennett

Sally Bennett's brushes with Bing were mostly fleeting but productive. Sally, a songwriter, playwright, model, actress, author, and radio and television hostess — I call her the Oprah Winfrey of Cleveland — always tried to get Bing to try out her songs. Sally is founder of the Big Band Hall of Fame in Palm Beach, Florida, where the bands, individual musicians, and vocalists are permanently showcased. Bing the vocalist, of course, was installed in the elite organization some time ago. Once, when Kathryn was performing summer theater in suburban Cleveland, Sally interviewed her and passed on a few songs for her to bring to Bing, and to respectfully invite Kathryn to become an Honorary Board Member of the Big Band Hall of Fame, sharing a place on the roster with Joe Franklin, George Hamilton, Curt Gowdy, Hoagy Bix Carmichael, Bob Hope, Donald Trump, Burt Reynolds, Merv Griffin, and Celia Lipton Farris. Sally and her husband Paul are quintessential Bing fans happy to count Bing as a revered member of their organization.

....
Sally Bennett
....

Roy Chappell
Crooning in the Crosby groove

by Max Wirz.

"I thought I heard Bing singing."

When Roy Chappell first met legendary Bing Crosby at Belle Vue, Manchester, England in 1977 and Bing learned that Roy sang some of his songs, the great man said, "Keep up the good work, Roy."

Author's Note: Max Wirz is a respected Big Band radio host from Switzerland who communicates enthusiastically about the great American music of the golden age, which includes the career of Bing Crosby. He contributed to my books The Music Men and Jukebox Saturday Night, writing extensively about the big bands of Europe and England. Max is a unique individual and a premium dispenser of American music. When told about the advent of this book, he suggested he locate a true Crosby link from Europe, a fellow named Roy Chappell. Max sat down with Roy and came up with this very interesting story:

Roy Chappell today (courtesy Roy Chappell)

On a balmy evening in Zurich, Switzerland during the summer of 1995, I strolled toward the Parade Platz to listen to a jazz band performance, when I thought I heard Bing Crosby singing. But, this was a live performance on a small stage. As I came closer, I noticed a singer in front of an eight piece band: hat on head, pipe in hand, tweed jacket, sport pants and two-tone wing-tipped shoes. He was singing Bing Crosby songs and sounded like Bing himself.

I should have paid more attention, because it was shortly later that I established my disc jockey

March 11, 1944

Dear Master Peacock:

Due to material shortages, I'm not going to be able to send out any more photos for the duration. It's almost impossible to obtain photo stock envelopes or card boards and I'm saving what we have to take care of the requests of the boys and girls in the different services.

I'm sure you'll bear with me in this until Victory is ours, and we can settle down again in peaceful living.

Our next picture is "Going My Way". Leo McCarey is the director, and Burke and Van Heusen, whose Dixie tunes are doing so well, wrote the score.

Yours for VICTORY,

Bing Crosby

BC:jl

At Gonzaga University 1981 – Bing Crosby Statue Unveiling. L to R. Phil Harris, Roy and Jimmy Van Heusen

show with Radio Thurgau, presenting *It's Showtime*, music from films and big bands. A short time later I saw an ad in *Jazztime*, the Swiss jazz bible, offering a CD entitled "Memories of Bing Crosby" and showing a picture of the fellow I heard sing that day in Zurich. His name was Roy Chappell. He had recorded with Harry Strutters Hot Rhythm Orchestra. I said to myself, *someday I will have to find this Roy Chappell guy, who sings like Bing Crosby, to interview for my show.*

That someday was practically forced upon me when author Richard Grudens sent me an e-mail to advise me of a forthcoming book about Bing Crosby saying, "If you can offer any help, please do." That someday was here. I quickly located the producer of the CD and obtained Roy Chappell's whereabouts. We became acquainted and exchanged CDs and other materials, and I told him of a needed interview for the book.

Roy Chappell was born in 1934 in Ashton-under-Lyne, near Manchester. Being near the same age, we got along very well reminiscing about the music following World War II. His real name was Roy Peacock and as a young man in 1944 he had written to Bing asking for a photo. Bing replied as follows: (see letter)

During his youth the family always played Bing on the radio. His Mom and Dad, Lily and Arthur Peacock, would sing Crosby style songs like "When I Lost You," an Irving Berlin tune recorded on July 20, 1940, and "Stardust," which Bing recorded four times over the years. Roy and his dad would sing duets of Bing's standards together while working on his Dad's vintage motor bike.

Roy cultivated an interest in dirt bikes and was featured in a national magazine as a coming speedway star, becoming the youngest rider in England and an apprentice in a car body and paint shop. He raced on just about every English Speedway. After a debilitating accident on a track, Roy decided to abandon his racing days. It was then that Roy Chappell, the singer, emerged onto the music scene.

Roy also listened to the American Forces Network in Europe, known as the AFN, who played Kay Starr, Doris Day, Peggy Lee, and Bing Crosby. The movies were *Holiday Inn*, *The Jolson Story*, and *White Christmas*, with all those beautiful songs we all loved. These were the influences on Roy.

ROY: "We used to go to the picture shows which featured mainly American musicals and the John Wayne and Jimmy Cagney films. My dad said, 'Go and see the *Jolson Story*, you'll like it!' And I did. I spent all my pocket money to see the early and late shows every day. By the end of the week I knew all Larry Parks gestures and every Al Jolson song by heart."

Roy absorbed all the sounds and songs he needed. the songs of Guy Mitchell, Frankie Laine's and Bing Crosby and came up with an idea. His dad altered his son's name to Al Phillips because the name Peacock was an invitation to hecklers to make fun of his name. He entered his son in a singing competition and *Al Phillips* was announced as the winner.

ROY: "I was quite successful and got to sing around different places in Manchester. The audiences like my interpretations of the great singers, especially Bing Crosby's songs. My voice had developed much like Bing's. But the bandleader Sid Phillips did not fancy having another *Phillips* on stage, so suggested we keep the *Roy*, but replace the last name. One night at a performance where he was to introduce me, he noticed a name on the underside of the piano cover, and blurted out *Roy Chappell*."

Roy Chappell performed his songs throughout Northwest England, also supporting himself by driving a beverage delivery van. "I could listen to music and sing all day and made a

Original
BCHS label
of mini-LP

pretty good living." He loved singing songs like Bing's version of "Did You Ever See a Dream Walking," and Frankie Laine's "Lucky Old Sun," reminding me of Frankie Laine's own struggle to enter show business.

Roy caught some of Bing's appearances and even obtained an autograph or two. On September 23, 1977, less than a month before Bing died in Spain, Roy's important time with Bing had arrived. Bing was to appear at the Kings Hall Belle-Vue Amusement Park in Manchester. A neighbor, Lawrence Stokes, a security guard at Kings Hall, was able to access Roy to the backstage bar area. When Bing and Kathryn came through, Kathryn stopped and ordered a mixture of orange and lemon and requested no one smoke back stage. Tommy Taylor, the Crosby's driver, knew Roy and was able to get him to meet Bing. He introduced Roy to Bing, and told him about his career and that he was plugging his songs in his act around England. "Thanks," Bing said "Keep up the good work." Someone took a photo and the two chatted a bit, then Bing excused himself to prepare for his performance. Roy was thrilled.

Bing allowed Roy to see the script and ran down his part to be played with Rosemary Clooney. Suddenly the lights went out. Bing said, "I hope it's not a bomb scare," and they continued their talking. Then Bing Crosby was called to the stage, which was built over a portion of the seats at one end. To access the stage, performers had to climb a steep stairway to a platform that led to center stage. The security guard kept close to Bing and they all climbed the stairs. Bing Crosby found the spotlight and they returned to the theater area to watch the show. That was an experience of a lifetime for Roy Chappell. He had met his hero, the father of his own career.

On May 3, 1980, Roy Chappell attended the unveiling of the Bing Crosby bronze statue at Gonzaga University in Spokane, Washington, having been invited by Ken Twiss, President of the Bing Crosby Historical Society.

"Prior to the ceremony, Kathryn Crosby asked me to sing a few songs with an organ backup. I sang five Bing songs and she must have been pleased. When photos were taken, Mrs. Crosby came towards me to shake my hand and said, 'That was very nice singing. Thank you very much for doing a tribute for Bing. I noticed, too, that you have your own style as well.'" Roy did not have a rehearsal for this impromptu performance.

During the visit Roy met with Mary Rose Pool, Bing's sister, and Rich Little, the impressionist who was a friend to Bing. Mary Rose was apprehensive about speaking at the event. "So am I," said Roy, which calmed her. "Just go up and take a bow. And she did just that. We chatted a bit and we kept in touch up until she passed. She once sent me a card saying that her brother Bob Crosby liked my recordings." Roy also met up

with Bing's friends Phil Harris and composer Jimmy Van Heusen. All were amazed at Roy's ability to sound so Bing-like.

Roy Chappell has since pursued an active career singing and has received favorable reviews. He has performed with many bands, including the great Syd Lawrence Orchestra. Recently, when the film *High Society* was shown at a local cinema, Roy was asked to sing a few Crosby style songs, backed up by Michael Holms on the organ. Malcolm Macfarlane, editor of the International Crosby Circle Magazine, was in the audience and wrote a favorable review. Further, the organist and Roy are producing a selection of Crosby songs for a forthcoming CD. Roy's CD "Memories of Bing Crosby" performed with Harry Strutters Hot Rhythm Orchestra, which specializes in the jazz and hot dance music of the '20s and '30s, became a hit in England as this book went to press. It was originally produced by the Bing Crosby Historical Society for the second "Tribute to Bing in Tacoma" held on May 3, 1980. Roy's business card reads, "A Bit of the Bing." In a letter to Roy, Ken Twiss wrote, "Frankly, your contribution at the Tribute was the highlight of the evening and I thoroughly enjoyed every minute of it."

Roy's deep intonations and rich voice reminds me of Bing Crosby, especially on "Darn That Dream." He surely evokes the sound of 1950s and 1960s Bing. Remarkable. Although he maintains he has not set out to imitate, Roy has always been a devoted follower of Bing and this has been his inspiration.

Bing Assesses his Career in a 1974 Interview

"We had a musical family. My sisters played the piano, my father played the mandolin and guitar, my mother sang in local theatricals. We always had music in the house. I guess we sang since we were very small, and it was kind of natural for me to be in a band and follow through with a career that has lasted all my life. I kind of developed my singing patterned after my hero Al Jolson. I learned a lot from him and the others I enjoyed at the time.

"I didn't, of course, earn much in the beginning. But I was content to be in an environment and around people I'd read about and heard about and whose records I'd listened to. I had no specific goals, I just wanted to be a part of it. I found myself in the company of jazz greats — Armstrong, the Dorsey Brothers, Beiderbecke, people like that. Those were my idols, you know — like Glenn Miller....and they all became my friends. Some friends, huh!"

By 1974 Bing was a long-established, bona fide living legend. Like most icons, he found it somewhat difficult to keep private and public life separated. He had always managed to keep his public image low-keyed and untarnished, unlike celebrities like Frank Sinatra, who always maintained a strong public image. Bing was now seventy years old with a lovely, talented, wife with cover girl looks, and three grown, very nice kids, all who adored him, as did his first four boys with Dixie. He walked with spunk and constantly sang or whistled and was always planning a trip here or there, somewhere in the world, for sports or entertainment.

People who knew Bing at that time said he was no longer a man seeking new ideas, politics, or anything old versus new. His home was a showplace with not much memorabilia to view. He readily commented about his life as a singer and actor:

"For me, the road to fame was mostly fun — a lot of laughs, very few hard bumps." Bing's book, written in 1953, was entitled "Call Me Lucky." He believed he was lucky to the end.

So, how did Bing spend his life in later years?

"I spend eighty or ninety days a year working — doing TV specials, fishing and hunting shows, guest spots, and a golf tournament or two. I eat well, get up at about five in the morning, and look forward to meeting old friends in the romantic marshes for the calls of wild ducks and geese, where we trade jokes and stories."

Once, Bing and some friends leased an island off Richmond, stocked it with quail and pheasant and hunted there for a few seasons. With friends he went deep sea fishing off his Las Cruces, Baja, Mexico hacienda, also sharing quality time there with Kathryn and their three youngsters.

In a September, 1954 letter to his friend and musical director John Scott Trotter, Bing reveals his concern then about his future as a singer. Bing was a widower, but had already met Kathryn, and, as we know, was a little mixed up and uncertain about his future, personal and professional:

"...I, of course, John, feel pretty sad about not going back on the radio this season. I have given many reasons for this decision to many different people, but I feel I can tell you the truth and that you will believe and understand me. John, I don't sing anywhere as good as I used to, and I feel sincerely that it's getting worse. I don't see any purpose in trying to stretch something out that was once acceptable and that now is merely adequate, if that. I don't know what the reason for this condition is, unless it's apathy. I just don't have the interest in singing. I am not keen about it any more. Songs all sound alike to me, and some of them so shoddy and trivial. I don't mean I didn't sing some cheap songs and bad songs in the old days, but I had such a tremendous interest in singing and was so wrapped up in the work that it didn't matter. I don't know how to diagnose the condition, but it seems to me that possibly this apathy, this lack of desire, when I have to go to a recording session, transmits itself into nervous exhaustion and fatigue......"

This certainly seemed like the beginning of the end of Bing's tremendous confidence. The words and expressions were clear. But it may have been an emotional transition, or feelings of loneliness, or thoughts of his own mortality, continuing after the loss of Dixie Lee in 1952. When this letter was written, he had begun a questionable, though remarkable and emotional relationship with young Kathryn Grandstaff that later reinforces his life and career and would become for him a life saving, stabilizing, happy marriage.

Of course, Bing sang beautifully in one of his best films, *White Christmas*, which he had finished earlier in the year, followed by *High Society* two years later in 1956, hardly depicting a man in crisis.

Epilogue

How do we account for Bing Crosby's immense success? Where lies the rationale? Admittedly an ordinary guy, not handsome or macho and not particularly focused on a singing career, he admits that entering show business was, for him, simply a good idea, realizing he could enjoy himself by singing and being involved in a pleasant career and earn probably more than a lawyer would've been paid in his day had he completed his studies. The work of singing songs was clearly easier to perform than practicing law.

Bing Crosby was an absolute original: self-confident, but not egotistical. He accomplished without formality what many others only dreamed about, as they may have performed their songs in the shower, at home parties, or church skits, never daring to take that radical step. Bing brought his abilities unabashedly to the heights of show business' greatest stages by just being himself. The world was apparently ready for this genuinely relaxed, cheerful, offhand, shoulder shrugging, low keyed performer who added his own signature "scat" technique, unknown to singers of his time.

Did he possess talent? Yes.

Was he a product of publicity? Some.

Was he lucky? Very.

What about competition? There was little. His approach was new and accepted.

Did the advent of the microphone contribute to his success? Quite a bit, although it usually was reflected in recordings.

His husky intonations of the time were a result of over-exhaustion from being up all night and possibly even hungover now and then by the time he reached the studio in the morning, but it added to his success.

Consider too, the mystique of those early Sennett filmshorts. Here, Sennett portrays Bing as the all-American boy next door. No competition with the ladies allowed by other suitors in the film, Bing receiving, without explanation, the undying, unearned affection and devotion of all featured ladies, young or middle-aged. Film fans, unsuccessful suitors in real life, observe for the first time an example of how simply the Crosby mystique is unveiled before their eyes. Casual crooning is served up, an outcry of a selfless performance by our hero, pipe smoking Bing Crosby, who is satirically wooing each film's ingenue by delivering to each one the seductive words of his songs, like other's expression of poetry heretofore served up, now converted to *crooning* a love story instead in a new and different way. Crosby was the new, heralded catalyst delivered through films, recordings, and radio, an excellent combination of vehicles.

And don't forget "time and chance" which happens to all.

His songs, with added improvisation: begged for love; pleaded for another chance; had the world on a string; had him crying again while waiting for someone at the gold of the day; surrendered to love; were through with love; apologized; were sorry, dear!

His songs exemplified open, personal expressions at a time when mostly Italian and Irish tenors operatically dispensed little involving film fans personal interests, something Bing took on and mastered beautifully. Success must also be attributed to great songwriting. After all, had there been no songs, there would have been no *Crosby*. The old tunes would simply not have cut it. Something had to happen: Crosby happened and *Time and Chance* happened for him.

Remember, too, that sound (talking and singing) films were relatively new. Jolson introduced film singing and Crosby personalized it. Songwriters began writing for crooners like Crosby for both movies and record sessions, unlike those uncroonable songs written earlier for vaudeville and Broadway musical plays. Radio programs featuring singers were considered revolutionary. Listeners simply dialed in their favorite crooner singing their favorite songs and right in their own bedroom or living room.

Bing with Fred Astaire

Bing with Eddie Condon and
Johnny Mercer, 195`1

Bing with Jolson, 1947

Bing with "Pops" Whiteman, 1948

PART FOUR
The Lists

The Movies

1930 – King of Jazz
> Paul Whiteman Orchestra, John Boles, Rhythm Boys
> Mississippi Mud, So the Blackbirds and the Bluebirds
> Got Together, A Bench in the Park, and Happy Feet

1932 – The Big Broadcast
> Stuart Erwin, George Burns and Gracie Allen
> Where the Blue of the Night. Dinah, Here Lies Love,
> Please

1933 – College Humor
> Jack Oakie and Mary Carlisle
> Learn to Croon, Moonstruck, Down the Old Ox Road,
> Play Ball

1933 – Too Much Harmony
> Judith Allen and Jack Oakie
> Boo Boo Boo, Thanks, The Day You Came Along,
> Buckin' the Wind.

1933 – Going Hollywood
> Marion Davies, Fifi D'Orsay, Ned Sparks and Stuart
> Erwin
> Going Hollywood, After Sundown, We'll Make Hay
> While the Sun Shines, Temptation, Beautiful Girl and
> Our Big Love Scene

1934 – We're Not Dressing
> Carole Lombard, Leon Errol, Ethel Merman and Ray
> Milland
> Goodnight, Lovely Little Lady, I Positively Refuse to
> Sing, She Reminds Me of You, May I?, Love Thy
> Neighbor and Once In a Blue Moon

1934 – She Loves Me Not
> Kitty Carlisle and Miriam Hopkins
> I'm Hummin' I'm Whistlin' I'm Singin', Love in
> Bloom and Straight from the Shoulder

1935 – Here is My Heart
Kitty Carlisle and Roland Young
June in January, With Every Breath I Take and Love is Just Around the Corner

1935 – Mississippi
W.C. Fields and Joan Bennett
Swanee River, Down by the River, Soon and It's Easy to Remember

1935 – Two For Tonight
Joan Bennett and Mary Boland
Two for Tonight, I Wish I were Aladdin, From the Top of Your Head, Takes Two to Make a Bargain and Without a Word of Warning

1936 – Anything Goes
Ethel Merman, Charles Ruggles and Ida Lupino
You're the Top, My Heart and I, Sailor Beware and Moonburn

1936 – Rhythm on the Range
Frances Farmer, Bob Burns and Martha Raye
Empty Saddles, I Can't Escape from You, Roundup Lullaby and I'm An Old Cowhand

1936 – Pennies from Heaven
Madge Evans, Donald Meek, Edith Fellows and Louis Armstrong
Pennies from Heaven, One Two Button Your Shoe, Let's Call a Heart a Heart and So Do I.

1937 – Waikiki Wedding
Shirley Ross, Bob Burns, Martha Raye, Anthony Quinn and Leif Erikson
Sweet Leilani, Blue Hawaii, In a Little Hula Heaven and Sweet is the Word for You.

1937 – Double or Nothing
Mary Carlisle, Martha Raye, Andy Devine and William Frawley
Smarty, The Moon Got in My Eyes, It's the Natural Thing to Do and All You want to Do is Dance.

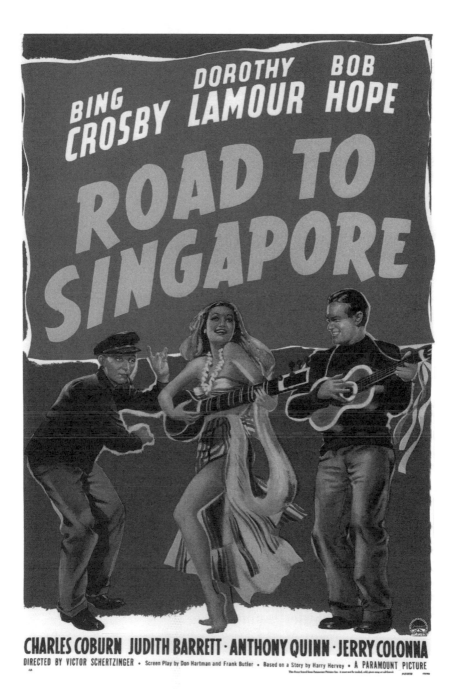

1938 – Doctor Rhythm
Mary Carlisle, Beatrice Lillie and Andy Devine
My Heart is Taking Lessons, On the Sentimental Side
and This is My Night to Dream

1938 – Sing You Sinners
Fred MacMurray and Donald O'Connor
I've Got a Pocketful of Dreams, Don't Let That Moon
Get Away, Laugh and Call it Love and Small Fry.

1939 – Paris Honeymoon
Franciska Gaal, Akim Tamiroff and Shirley Ross
I Have Eyes, You're a Sweet Little Headache, Funny
Old Hills and Joobalai.

1939 – East Side of Heaven
Joan Blondell and Mischa Auer
Happy Birthday, Sing a Song of Moonbeams, Hang
Your Heart on a Hickory Limb, that Sly Old
Gentlemen and East Side of Heaven

1939 – The Star Maker
Louise Campbell and Ned Sparks
Jimmy Valentine, A Man and His Dream, If I was a
Millionaire, Go Fly a Kite, I Wonder Who's Kissing
Her Now, In My Merry Oldsmobile, An Apple for the
Teacher, Schooldays, and
Still the Bluebird Sings.

1940 – Road to Singapore
Bob Hope, Dorothy Lamour, Charles Coburn,
Anthony Quinn and Jerry Colonna
Captain Custard, Too Romantic and Sweet Potato
Piper

1940 – If I Had My Way
Gloria Jean, Charles Winninger and El Brendel.
Meet the Sun Halfway, I Haven't Time to Be a
Millionaire, If I Had My Way, April Played the Fiddle
and Pessimistic Character.

1940 – Rhythm On the River
Mary Martin, Basil Rathbone and Oscar Levant
Rhythm On the River, Only Forever, What Would
Shakespeare Have Said, That's For Me and When the
Moon Comes Over Madison Square.

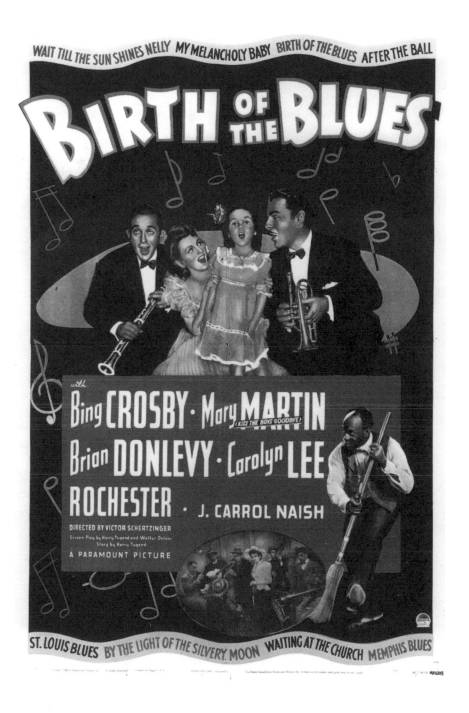

1941 – Road to Zanzibar
Bob Hope, Dorothy Lamour, Una Merkel and Eric Blore
You Lucky People You, It's Always You and On the Road to Zanzibar

1941 – Birth of the Blues
Mary Martin, Brian Donlevy, Carolyn Lee and Jack Teagarden
Birth of the Blues, By the Light of the Silvery Moon, Wait 'Til the Sun Shines Nelly, My Melancholy Baby, The Waiter and the Porter and the Upstairs Maid and St. Louis Blues.

1942 – Holiday Inn
Fred Astaire, Marjorie Reynolds, Virginia Dale and Walter Abel
I'll Capture Your Heart, White Christmas, Happy Holiday, Let's Start the New Year Right, Easter Parade, Abraham, Song of Freedom and I've Got Plenty to be Thankful For.

1942 – Road to Morocco
Bob Hope, Dorothy Lamour, Anthony Quinn and Dona Drake
Road to Morocco, Ain't Got a Dime to My Name and Moonlight Becomes You

1942 – Star Spangled Rhythm
Betty Hutton, Victor Moore, Eddie Bracken and Walter Abel
Old Glory

1943 – Dixie
Dorothy Lamour, Marjorie Reynolds and Billy De Wolfe
Sunday, Monday Or Always, Swing Low, Sweet Chariot, If You Please, Old Dan Tucker, She's from Missouri, A Horse That Knows the Way Back Home and Dixie.

1944 – Going My Way
Barry Fitzgerald, Frank McHugh, Stanley Clements, Rise' Stevens
Too-Ra-Loo-Ra-Loo-Ral, The Day After Forever, Going My Way, Ave Maria, Silent Night and Swinging On a Star

1944 – Here Comes the Waves
Betty Hutton, Sonny Tufts, Ann Doran and Gwen Crawford
That Old Black Magic, Let's Take the Long Way Home, Ac-Cent-Tchu-Ate the Positive, and I Promise You.

1945 – The Bells of St. Mary's
Ingrid Bergman, Henry Travers, Dickie Tyler and Joan Carroll
Aren't You Glad You're You, Adeste Fideles, In the Land of Beginning Again, O Sanctissima and The Bells of St.Mary's

1946 – The Road to Utopia
Bob Hope, Dorothy Lamour, Douglas Dumbrille and Jack LaRue
Goodtime Charlie, Welcome to My Dream, It's Anybody's Spring and Put It There Pal.

1946 – Blue Skies
Fred Astaire, Joan Caulfield, Billy DeWolfe and Olga San Juan
I've Got My Captain Working for Me Now, All By Myself, I'll See You in C-u-b-a, A Couple of Song and Dance Men, Blue Skies, Everybody Step, You Keep Coming Back Like a Song, Getting Nowhere, and Medley: Any Bonds Today, This is the Army, White Christmas.

1947 – Welcome Stranger
Barry Fitzgerald, Joan Caulfield and Wanda Hendrix
Smile Right Back at the Sun, Country Style, My Heart is a Hobo and As Long As I'm Dreaming.

1948 – The Emperor Waltz
Joan Fontaine, Roland Culver and Richard Haydn
I Kiss Your Hand Madam, The Kiss in Your Eyes, The Friendly Mountains and The Emperor Waltz

1948 – Road to Rio
Bob Hope, Dorothy Lamour, Gale Sondergaard and The Andrews Sisters
Apalachicola FLA, But Beautiful and You Don't Have to Know the Language

1949 – A Connecticut Yankee In King Arthur's Court
Rhonda Fleming, William Bendix and Sir Cedric
Hardwicke
If You Stub Your Toe on the Moon, Once and For
Always and Busy Doing Nothing.

1949 – Top O' the Morning
Barry Fitzgerald, Ann Blyth and Hume Cronyn
When Irish Eyes Are Smiling, Kitty of Coleraine, The
Donovans, You're In Love with Someone, Top O' the
Morning and O 'Tis Sweet to Think.

1950 – Riding High
Colleen Gray, Raymond Walburn, William Demarest,
Frances Gifford and Charles Bickford
Sure Thing, Someplace on Anywhere Road, Sunshine
Cake, The Horse Told Me and Camptown Races

1950 – Mr. Music
Nancy Olson, Charles Coburn, Robert Stack,Groucho
Marx, and Peggy Lee
And You'll Be Home, High On the List, Wouldn't It
Be Funny, Accidents Will Happen, Wasn't I There
and Life Is So Peculiar.

1951 – Here Comes the Groom
Jane Wyman, Franchot Tone and Alexis Smith
Your Own Little House, In the Cool, Cool, Cool of the
Evening, Misto Cristofo Columbo, O Promise Me and
Bonne Nuit.

1952 – Just for You
Jane Wyman, Bob Arthur, Natalie Wood, Cora
Witherspoon and Ethel Barrymore
I'll Si-Si Ya In Bahia, Zing a Little Zong, The Live
Oak Tree, On the Ten-Ten from Ten-Ten Tennessee
and Just for You

1953 – Road to Bali
Bob Hope, Dorothy Lamour and Murvyn Vye
Chicago Style, Whiffenpoof Song, Hoot Mon, To See
You Is to Love You and The Merry-Go-Run-Around.

IRVING BERLIN'S
VISTAVISION
White Christmas
COLOR BY TECHNICOLOR
STARRING
BING CROSBY · DANNY KAYE
ROSEMARY CLOONEY · VERA-ELLEN
with DEAN JAGGER · Lyrics and Music by IRVING BERLIN · Produced by Robert Emmett Dolan · Directed by MICHAEL CURTIZ
Dances and Musical Numbers Staged by Robert Alton · Written for the screen by Norman Krasna, Norman Panama and Melvin Frank
A PARAMOUNT PICTURE

1953 – Little Boy Lost
Nicole Maurey, Claude Dauphin and Christian
Fourcade
The Darktown Strutters Ball, A Propos De Rien, Cela
m'Est Egal (If It's All the Same to You) and The
Magic Window.

1954 – White Christmas
Danny Kaye, Rosemary Clooney, Vera Ellen, Dean
Jagger and Mary Wickes
Snow, Count Your Blessings, Mandy, I'd Rather See a
Minstrel Show, What Can You Do with a General,
Gee, I Wish I was Back in the Army, The Old Man
and White Christmas.

1954 – The Country Girl
Grace Kelly and William Holden
It's Mine It's Yours, The Search is Through, The Land
Around Us and Dissertation On the State of Bliss.

1956 – Anything Goes
Donald O'Connor, Jeanmaire, Mitzi Gaynor and Phil
Harris
Ya Gotta Give the People Hoke, You're the Top, All
Through the Night, A Second-Hand Turban and a
Crystal Ball and Blow, Gabriel Blow

1956 – High Society
Frank Sinatra, Grace Kelly, Louis Armstrong and
Celeste Holm
Little One, True Love, I Love You Samantha, Now
You Has Jazz and Well, Did You Evah.

1957 – Man On Fire
Inger Stevens, Mary Fickett and E.G. Marshall
Man On Fire

1959 – Say One for Me
Debbie Reynolds, Robert Wagner and Ray Walston
Say One for Me, I Couldn't Care less and The Secret
of Christmas

A NEW HIGH IN THE MOVIE SKY. M-G-M PRESENTS IN VISTAVISION AND COLOR
A SOL C. SIEGEL PRODUCTION

Starring

BING GRACE FRANK
CROSBY KELLY SINATRA

in the hilarious low-down on high life

co-starring

CELESTE HOLM · JOHN LUND

LOUIS CALHERN · SIDNEY BLACKMER

and **LOUIS ARMSTRONG** and His Band

Screen Play by JOHN PATRICK   Based on a Play by PHILIP BARRY

Music and Lyrics by **COLE PORTER**

Color by TECHNICOLOR   Directed by CHARLES WALTERS

1960 – High Time
Fabian, Tuesday Weld and Nicole Maurey
The Second Time Around, You Tell Me Your Dream
and It Came Upon a Midnight Clear

1962 – The Road to Hong Kong
Bob Hope, Dorothy Lamour, Joan Collins and Robert
Morley
Road to Hong Kong, Teamwork and Let's Not Be
Sensible

1964 – Robin and the Seven Hoods
Frank Sinatra, Dean Martin, Sammy Davis, Jr., Peter
Falk and Barbara Rush
Style, Mr. Booze and Don't Be a Do-Badder

1966 – Stagecoach
Ann Margret, Michael Connors, Alex Cord, Red
Buttons, Ven Heflin, Slim Pickens and Stephanie
Powers
No songs sung by Bing in this film

1974 – That's Entertainment
Bing as Narrator only in Part One

Film Notes: For five straight years, 1944-1949, Bing Crosby
was the Number one Box Office star. He won the Academy
Award in 1944 for *Going My Way* and was nominated Best
Actor for *The Bells of St.Mary's* in 1945 and for *The Country
Girl* in 1954. Bing appeared in 104 films that included his
Mack Sennett shorts and Paramount shorts, *Please* and *Just
an Echo*, the MGM short *Star Night at the Cocoanut Grove*,
and cameo appearances: *Reaching for the Moon, Confessions
of a Co-ed, The Big Broadcast of 1936, My Favorite Blonde,
Star Spangled Rhythm, The Princess and the Pirate, Duffy's
Tavern, Variety Girl, My Favorite Brunette, Angels in the
Outfield, The Greatest Show on Earth, Son of Paleface,
Scared Stiff, Alias Jesse James, Let's Make Love, Pepe,* and
Cancel My Reservation

Books About Bing

1946 – The Story of Bing Crosby by Ted Crosby
1946 – Bing Crosby and the Bing Crosby Style by Dr. J.T.H. Mize
1948 – The Incredible Crosby by Barry Ulanov
1953 – Call Me Lucky by Bing Crosby
1967 – Bing and Other Things by Kathryn Crosby
1973 – Bing Crosby -Cremo Singer by Larry F. Kiner
1975 – Bing by Charles Thompson
1977 – Bing – A Pyramid Illustrated History of the Movies by Barbara Bauer
1977 – The Fabulous Life of Bing Crosby by George Carpozi, Jr.
1977 – The Films of Bing Crosby by Robert Bookbinder
1977 – The One and Only Bing by Bob Thomas
1978 – Bing – A Lifetime of Music by Laurence J. Zwisohn
1978 – The Complete Crosby by Charles Thompson
1980 – Bing, Just for the Record by Bert Bishop and John Bassett
1980 – The Crosby Years by Ken Barnes
1980 – Philco Radio Time by Lionel Pairpoint
1981 – Bing Crosby; The Hollow Man by D.Shepherd and R.E. Slatzer
1983 – Going My Own Way by Gary Crosby and Ross Firestone
1983 – My Life with Bing by Kathryn Crosby
1984 – A Voice For All Seasons by Sheldon O'Connell
1986 – Road to Hollywood by Fred Reynolds
1986 – The Bing Crosby Show for General Electric by Lionel Pairpoint
1987 – List and Filmography by Timothy A. Morgereth
1987 – The Bing Crosby Show for Chesterfield – A Directory by Lionel Pairpoint
1988 – The Kraft Music Hall Starring Bing Crosby by Lionel Pairpoint
1988 – Alternate Bing Crosby by Colin Pugh
1992 – Jazz Singing by Will Friedwald
1994 – Bing Crosby; A Bio-Bibliography by J. Roger Osterholm

1996 – Bing Crosby A Songography by Frans W Vander Kolff
1996 – Bing Crosby In the 30s by G.D.Hamann
1996 – The Best Damn Trumpet Player by Richard Grudens
1996 – The Songs of Bing Crosby on Compact Disc by Jim Reilly
1997 – Bing Crosby In the 40s by G.D.Hamann
1997 – Bing – A Diary of a Lifetime by Malcolm Macfarlane
1998 – Bing Crosby In the 50s by G.D. Hamann
1998 – Bing Crosby the Illustrated Biography by Michael Freedland
1998 – The Music Men by Richard Grudens
2001 – A Pocketful of Dreams-The Early Years by Gary Giddins
2001 – Bing Crosby's Commercial Recordings by F.B. (Wig) Wiggins

The Best Songs

His Very Best — according to the author

1931 – I SURRENDER, DEAR
       WRAP YOUR TROUBLES IN DREAMS
       OUT OF NOWHERE
       JUST ONE MORE CHANCE
       I FOUND A MILLION DOLLAR BABY
       SWEET AND LOVELY
       WHERE THE BLUE OF THE NIGHT
       DINAH

Bing recording at Columbia, 1930
(courtesy Columbia)

1932 – ST. LOUIS BLUES
SHINE
LOVE IN BLOOM
STRAIGHT FROM THE SHOULDER
JUNE IN JANUARY
LOVE IS JUST AROUND THE CORNER
STREET OF DREAMS

1935 – IT'S EASY TO REMEMBER
RED SAILS IN THE SUNSET
SILENT NIGHT

1936 – I'M AN OLD COWHAND
SONG OF THE ISLANDS
PENNIES FROM HEAVEN

1937 – SWEET LEILANI
BLUE HAWAII
SMARTY
BOB WHITE

1938 – MY HEART IS TAKING LESSONS
HOME ON THE RANGE
YOU MUST HAVE BEEN A BEAUTIFUL BABY
YOU'RE A SWEET LITTLE HEADACHE
MY MELANCHOLY BABY

Laverne,
Bing, Patty
and Maxene
recording at
Decca, 1943
*(courtesy Patty
Andrews)*

1939 – MY ISLE OF GOLDEN DREAMS
CIRIBIRIBIN (with the Andrews Sisters)
YODELIN' JIVE (with the Andrews Sisters)

1940 – I HAVEN'T TIME TO BE A MILLIONAIRE
ONLY FOREVER
IF I HAD MY WAY
WHERE THE BLUE OF THE NIGHT
MEET THE SUN HALFWAY
RHYTHM ON THE RIVER
I FOUND A MILLION DOLLAR BABY
PLEASE
NEW SAN ANTONIO ROSE

1941 – BIRTH OF THE BLUES
THE WAITER AND THE PORTER AND THE
UPSTAIRS MAID
WAIT TIL THE SUN SHINES NELLIE

1942 – SKYLARK
LAZY
WHITE CHRISTMAS
HAPPY HOLIDAY
ROAD TO MOROCCO

1943 – PISTOL PACKIN' MAMA (with the Andrews
Sisters)
JINGLE BELLS (with the Andrews Sisters)
I'LL BE HOME FOR CHRISTMAS
VICT'RY POLKA (with the Andrews Sisters)

1944 – SWINGING ON A STAR
THE DAY AFTER FOREVER
GOING MY WAY
DEARLY BELOVED
DON'T FENCE ME IN (with the Andrews
Sisters)
EVELINA
LET ME CALL YOU SWEETHEART
ROAD TO MOROCCO
AC-CENT-TCHU-ATE THE POSITIVE (with
the Andrews Sisters)

1945 – BAIA
        YOU BELONG TO MY HEART
        ALONG THE NAVAJO TRAIL (with the
        Andrews Sisters)
        TOO-RA-LOO-RA-LOO-RAL
        AVE MARIA
        IN THE LAND OF BEGINNING AGAIN
        THE BELL'S OF ST. MARY'S
        MCNAMARA'S BAND
        AREN'T YOU GLAD YOU'RE YOU
        SIOUX CITY SUE

1946 – A GAL IN CALICO
        SOUTH AMERICA, TAKE IT AWAY (with the
        Andrews Sisters)
        ALL BY MYSELF
        I'LL SEE YOU IN C-U-B-A
        COUNTRY STYLE
        MY HEART IS A HOBO

1947 – FRIENDLY MOUNTAINS
        THE CHRISTMAS SONG
        KOKOMO, INDIANA
        THE FREEDOM TRAIN
        YOU DON'T HAVE TO KNOW THE LAN-
        GUAGE (with the Andrews Sisters)
        APALACHICOLA, F-L-A (with the Andrews
        Sisters)
        GALWAY BAY
        ONCE AND FOR ALWAYS
        HAUNTED HEART

1948 – FAR AWAY PLACES

1949 – SUNSHINE CAKE
        THE FIRST NOEL
        WAY BACK HOME
        DEAR HEARTS AND GENTLE PEOPLE

1950 – HIGH ON THE LIST (with the Andrews Sisters)
        JAMBOREE JONES
        PLAY A SIMPLE MELODY (with Gary Crosby)

SAM'S SONG (with Gary Crosby)
HARBOR LIGHTS
MELE KALIKIMAKA (with the Andrews Sisters)
SILVER BELLS

1951 – GONE FISHIN'
IN THE COOL, COOL, COOL OF THE
EVENING
MISTO CHRISTOFO COLUMBO
IT'S BEGINNING TO LOOK A LOT LIKE
CHRISTMAS

1952 – I'LL SI-SI YA IN BAHIA
ZING A LITTLE ZONG

1953 – THE MAGIC WINDOW
CELA M'EST EGAL
VIOLETS AND VIOLINS

1954 – SNOW
COUNT YOUR BLESSINGS
1955 – MOST SONGS AFTER THIS DATE WERE
REPEATS IN ALBUMS AND RE-ISSUES.

MAY 1989

Number 44

THE
CROONER

THE BING CROSBY HISTORICAL SOCIETY
Tacoma, Washington, U.S.A. - Bing's Birthplace

BINGTHINGS by Bob Lundberg

Interesting Crosbyana

Bob Lundberg wrote a feature about Bing Crosby which he named BINGTHINGS, and it appeared in the "Crooner," the newsletter of The Bing Crosby Historical Society of Tacoma, Washington, where Bing was born. Bob Lundberg continued his column after Ken Twiss passed on, naming his organization "The Bingthings Society," which he managed with his wife Joyce.His column was re-named "Bingtalks" which he wrote until his own passing.

> *Here are some samples of Bob Lundberg's Bingthings:*
> *B I N G T H I N G S*
> *Some you may know — some you may not!*
>
> By Bob Lundberg

Bing scored 38 Number One hits during his career. The Beatles had 24 Number one hits and Elvis Presley had but 18.

Between 1927 and 1962, Bing charted 368 recordings under his own name and 28 more as a vocalist with other bands for a total of 396 charted discs. Frank Sinatra had 209, Elvis had 149, Nat King Cole had 118 and the Beatles had 68.

By 1980 Bing sold more than 400 million recordings when very few had phonographs or enough money to purchase recordings. Bing's recording of "White Christmas," recorded on May 29, 1942 (also Bob Hope's birthday), is the most popular, best selling, single voice recording in history. It made the charts 20 times between 1942 and 1962 for a total of 50 million copies sold. If you add in LPs and CDs, it tops over 100 million.

Bing made over 2,600 commercial recordings.

Bing's first Gold Record was "Sweet Leilani" from the film *Waikiki Wedding* in 1937. The song won the Academy Award.

Bing's LP "Bing's Hollywood Collection" is the biggest LP release ever sold with 189 songs on 15 LP 12" records.

Movies

In 1946, three of the top five grossing films *The Bells of St. Mary's*, *Blue Skies*, and *Road to Utopia* were Bing Crosby vehicles.

Bing is the third most popular movie star in the history of films.

For 5 years running, 1944 through 1948, Bing was the No. 1 Box Office star.

Bing's radio shows from 1931 through 1962 peaked with 50 million listeners to one show.

Bing was born on May 3, 1903. He always believed he was born on May 2, 1904. Ken Twiss of The Bing Crosby Historical Society proved it by locating and producing Bing's Baptismal Certificate.

Bing's favorite desert was German Chocolate cake.

Bing enjoyed reading works by authors Ernest Hemingway, John Steinbeck, "Ring" Lardner, W. Somerset Maugham and Aldous Huxley.

Bing's 1971 televised Pro-Am Golf Tournament still holds the record for the largest audience ever for a golf event.

Bing and his brother Everett were colorblind, which accounts for Bing's flashy, yet confusing choices of color in his clothing. He was known to wear brown socks with black suits. He once thanked fellow actor Richard Arlen for a purple and red polka-dotted shirt saying, "Thanks for the beautiful yellow shirt."

Bing's sobriquet "Der Bingle" was coined by the Nazi's during World War II.

Bing's net worth on October 18, 1948 was listed in *Newsweek Magazine* as being $1,649,115.00.

Bing was listed in *Life Magazine* as one of the *100 Most Important Americans of the 20th Century.*

Bing's first great hit in motion pictures occurred in 1934 in the film *She Loves Me Not.* The tune "Love Thy Neighbor," stayed in the Top Ten for twelve weeks. "She Reminds Me of You," "Once in a Blue Moon," and "Good Night, Lovely Little Lady," were the other tunes from the film.

"Your Hit Parade" was a weekly broadcast of the top tunes that began on April 20, 1935. The first number one tune on the first broadcast was Bing's song from *Mississippi* entitled "Soon." Another song from the same film "It's Easy to Remember," also made the list.

Bing's nickname, "The Groaner," derived from his time with Paul Whiteman. It originated while he sang with the band and was coined by Tommy Dorsey, the band's trombonist, later known as the "Sentimental Gentleman of Swing."

BING

AUGUST
1996

No. 113

THE INTERNATIONAL CROSBY CIRCLE

....

The magazine "Bing"

....

Bing's voice has been heard by more people than any other voice in history.

When Bing performed 20 consecutive weeks at the New York Paramount, his fan mail soared to 7,500 pieces of mail each month.

Bing was honored by *Look Magazine* on March 30, 1955 with the Best Actor Award for *The Country Girl* bestowed upon him by television comedian Red Skelton.

In 1937, June, Bing was named "Hollywood's Most Typical Father."

Bing's Clubs

There have been and still are a number of Bing Crosby fan clubs, the oldest being Club Crosby founded in 1936 in the state of Maine and now located in Kirkwood, Mo. Managed by its President, Mark Scrimger, and Wayne Martin, its Vice President. Kathryn is their Honorary President. The club's European representative is Ken Crossland, located in England. The Bing Crosby Historical Society was founded by Ken Twiss after Bing's death and disbanded in 1993 upon his passing. Its holdings were sent to Bing's alma mater, Gonzaga University's Student Center, the former Library, where Bing is well represented. Formed in 1981 Bing's Friends and Collector Society is under the management of Cathie and Hobie Wilson since its inception. The International Crosby Circle, founded in 1950, is located in England. Michael Crampton is the Secretary and Malcolm Macfarlane is the magazine editor. The very active United States Representative is F.B. "Wig" Wiggins who resides in Arlington, Virginia. All these clubs publish excellent newsletters several times a year. Bob Lundberg and Joyce Lundberg, formerly of the defunct Historical Society,formed The Bingthings Society, but it disbanded upon Bob's passing.

BING'S STAMP

After many years of trying to persuade the United States Postal Service to issue a stamp with Bing's likeness on it, Ken Twiss and other Crosby fans and fan clubs finally won their battle. "If they can feature Elvis on a stamp, they sure could present Bing," said Ken. A Bing Crosby stamp was issued on September 1, 1994. Kenneth Symbol, Jr., Postmaster of Spokane, Washington, wrote to confirm its issuance. I, along

UNITED STATES POSTAL SERVICE

From the office of Postmaster Kenneth S. Symbol, Jr.
904 W. Riverside Ave. • PO Box 79 • Spokane, WA 99210-0079
(509) 626-6850 • FAX (509) 626-6919

August 19, 1994

I would like to take this opportunity to invite you to a very special event
being held in Spokane on September 1st at 11:00 a.m. in front of the
Crosby Student Center on the campus of Gonzaga University.

At that time the United States Postal Service and the Spokane Post
Office, in conjunction with Gonzaga University, will hold a dedication
ceremony for the Popular Singers Stamps with special emphasis on the
Bing Crosby Stamp. After the ceremony there will be a special pictorial
cancellation of the stamps as well as a tour of the Crosby Collection.

Bing Crosby never forgot his hometown of Spokane and during his
lifetime made many visits here to renew his roots and show his
appreciation for the people of this area. We are proud to be able to show
our high regard to this man and his life.

I hope you will be able to join us for this very special day.

Sincerely,

Kenneth Symbol, Jr
Postmaster

with other club members received an invitation to attend a ceremony to be held at the Crosby Student Center on the campus of Gonzaga. The dedication ceremony for the Popular Singers Stamp Series was punctuated by a special pictorial cancellation of the stamp. A great day for all Crosby fans officially commemorating Bing so all could be aware of his magnificent musical legacy.

Parker Brothers' Bing game

Acknowledgements

First, thanks must be expressed to all the Crosby Clubs, past and present, whose hard work and vision have kept Bing Crosby's legacy alive: The Bing Crosby Historical Society, Club Crosby, Bingthings Society, International Bing Crosby Circle, Bing's Friends and Collectors Society; and individually: the late Ken Twiss and Bob Lundberg, Joyce Lundberg, Hobie and Cathy Wilson, Wig Wiggins, Charles Baillie, Greg Van Beek, Ernest Sutkowski, Vern Taylor, Malcolm Macfarlane, David Lobosco, Jeff Geist, Bill Morrow, Mark Scrimger, Pete Cakanic, Nat Hentoff, Gord Atkinson, and specialist Ron Hall.

Special thanks to the magnificent Kathryn Crosby, Phillip Crosby, Patty Andrews, Jerry Vale, Jack Ellsworth, Bob Hope, Les Paul, Connie Haines, Rhonda Fleming, Joe Franklin, Roy Chappell, Gloria Jean, and all who have recently contributed their accounts.

Personal help from friends: Frankie Laine, my personal mentor who helped get me started, Swiss jazz broadcaster and journalist Max Wirz, idea advisors Jerry Castleman and Bob Incagliato, my late, great photographers C.Camille Smith and Gus Young, broadcaster and advisor Al Monroe, bandleader and musical advisor Ben Grisafi, music historian and human music library Joe Pardee, my brand new editor, Kristi Watson, straight from fresh Masters Degree Recipient from Adelphi University, and Anthony DiFlorio III, who has always been there with his insight and advice. Special Mention for my son, Bob, my best all around assistant.

....

"Wig" Wiggins
(International Crosby Circle)

....

Bibliography

Bach, Bob and Ginger Mercer, *Our Huckleberry Friend*, Secaucus, New Jersey: Lyle Stuart, Inc. 1982

Bauer, Barbara. *Bing Crosby-A Pyramid Illustrated History of the Movies*. New York, New York: Pyramid Publications, 1977

Beck, *Endpaper 3.17.02*, New York Times Magazine: New York, New York, New York Times, 2002

Cagney, James. *Cagney by Cagney*, New York, New York: Doubleday Book Company, 1976

Carpozi, Jr. *The Fabulous Life of Bing Crosby*, New York, New York: Manor Books, Inc. 1977

Crosby, Kathryn. *Bing and Other things*. New York, New York: Meredith Press, 1967

Crosby, Kathryn, *My Life with Bing*, Wheeling, Illinois: Collage, Inc. 1983

Crosby, Bing, with Pete Martin. *Call Me Lucky*. New York, New York: Simon and Shuster, 1953

Crosby, Ted. *The Story of Bing Crosby*. New York, New York: The World Publishing Company, 1946

Grudens, Richard. *The Best Damn Trumpet Player*. Stonybrook, New York: Celebrity Profiles Publishing, 1996.

Grudens, Richard, *The Music Men*. Stonybrook, New York: Celebrity Profiles Publishing, 1998

Grudens, Richard, *Bing Crosby's Legacy*, California Highway Patrolman Magazine, August 1989

Laine, Frankie,and Joseph F. Laredo, *That Lucky Old Son*. Ventura, California: Pathfinder Publishing, 1993.

Lee, Peggy, *Miss Peggy Lee, An Autobiography*, New York, New York: Donald I. Fine, 1989

Lundberg, Bob & Joyce, Charles Baillie, *Bingtalk*s, Bingthings Society Newsletter, Tacoma, Washington: 1990-1999

Martin, Wayne, Editor, *Bingang*, Club Crosby, Kirkwood, Missouri. 1936 — 2002

Macfarlane, Malcolm, Editor *Bing Magazine* International Crosby Circle. Cheshire, England. Current and past dates.

Osterholm, J. Roger, *Bing Crosby A Bio-Bibliography*, Westport, Connecticut: Greenwood Press, 1994

Ross, Adalene. *Kathryn Crosby Interview*, Family Circle Magazine, December 1977

Simon, George T., *Glenn Miller and His Orchestra*, New York, New York: Thomas Y. Crowell Company 1974

Sforza, John. *Swing It — The Andrew Sisters Story*, Lexington, Kentucky: The University Press of Kentucky, 2000

Thompson, Charles. *Bing – The Authorized Biography*, New York, New York: David McKay Company, Inc. 1975

Tormé, Mel. *It Wasn't All Velvet*, New York, New York: Viking Penquin, 1988.

Tormé, Mel. *My Singing Teachers*, New York, New York: Oxford University Press, 1994

Ken Twiss, Bill Osborn, Bob Lundberg, *The Crooner*, Bing Crosby Historical Society Newsletter, Tacoma, Washington, 1980-1990

Walker, Leo. *The Wonderful Era of the Great Dance Bands*. New York, New York: DaCapo Press, Inc., 1964

Walker, Leo. *The Big Band Almanac*, Hollywood, California: Vinewood Enterprises, Inc. 1978.

Wiggins, F.B. *Bing Crosby's Commercial Recordings*, Arlington, Virginia, Self-Published 2001

Wilson, Cathy & Hobie, *Bing's Friends and Collectors Society Newsletter*, Sonoma,California. 1985-1999

RICHARD GRUDENS

100th
BIRTHDAY
EDITION

THE SPIRIT OF

BOB HOPE

★ *One Hundred Years* ★ *One Million Laughs* ★

Foreword by Jane Russell

Bob's Book • Bing's In It!

Thanks

Camille Smith

Al Monroe

Joe Pardee

Max Wirz

Connie Haines

Jerry Castleman

Ben Grisafi

Bob DeBetta

Bob Incagliato

Kristi Watson

Jerry Vale and Richard Grudens at
Radio Station WALK 2002

Frankie Laine and Richard Grudens
at Westbury Music Fair, 1992

Larry O'Brien, Glenn Miller Band
Leader, Connie Haines and Richard
Grudens, Three Village Inn, 2001

Max Wirz of Radio EVIVA, Switzerland
visits author for Roy Chappell chapter

About the Author

Richard Grudens of Stony Brook, New York, was initially influenced by Pulitzer Prize dramatist Robert Anderson; *New York Herald Tribune* columnist Will Cuppy; and detective/mystery writer Dashiell Hammett, all whom he knew in his early years. Grudens worked his way up from a studio page in NBC's studios in New York to news writer for such news shows as H.V. Kaltenborn, John Cameron Swayze, Bob & Ray and "The Today Show".

Feature writing for *Long Island P.M. Magazine* (1980-86) led to his first book, *The Best Damn Trumpet Player—Memories of the Big Band Era*. He has written over 100 magazine articles on diverse subjects from interviews with legendary cowboy Gene Autry in *Wild West Magazine* in 1995 to a treatise on the Beach Boys in the *California Highway Patrol Magazine*, and countless articles on Bing Crosby, Bob Hope, including a major Bob Hope cover article about Hope's famous USO tours, published in *World War Magazine*. He has written extensively about Henry Ford, VE Day, Motorcycle Helmet Safety, DNA history, among other subjects.

His other books include *The Song Stars*—about the girl singers (1997); *The Music Men*—about the men singers (1998); *Jukebox Saturday Night*—more memories of the Big Band Era (1999); *Snootie Little Cutie—The Connie Haines Story*, and *Magic Moments—The Sally Bennett Story* (2000), *Jerry Vale—A Singer's Life* (2001), "The Spirit of Bob Hope" (2002).

Commenting about the book *Jukebox Saturday Night* in 1999, Kathryn (Mrs. Bing) Crosby wrote, *"Richard Grudens is the musical historian of our time. Without him, the magic would be lost forever. We all owe him a debt that we can never repay."*

EXPLORE the GOLDEN AGE OF MUSIC when the Big Bands and their vocalists reigned on the radio and all the the great stages of America.

SIX GREAT BOOKS
BY RICHARD GRUDENS

INDEX

Pied Pipers, 54
Pierson, Al, 54
Pinera, Manuel, 95
Pinza, Ezio, 122
Phillips, Sid, 201
Polesie, Midge, 47
Porter, Cole, 111, 168
Presley, Elvis, 55, 176

Q
Quinn, Anthony, 162

R
Rainger, Ralph, 144, 145
Reynolds, Burt, 197
Reynolds, Marjorie, 148
Rhythm Boys, The, 16, 18, 19, 23, 102, 148
Rich, Buddy, 170
Rinker, Al, 10-13, 15, 16, 22, 26, 122, 125, 186
Robin, Leo, 144, 145
Rodgers and Hart, 174
Rodgers & Hammerstein, 111, 122
Rogers, Ted, 93, 189
Romano, Tony, 123
Ross, Shirley, 21, 126, 145
Rush, Art, 76
Russell, Andy, 21, 126, 172
Russell, Jane, 194
Russin, Jack, 131

S
Sandrich, Mark, 148
Schoen, Vic, 117
Seabiscuit, 48, 89
Sennett, Mack, 25-27, 30, 207
Shaw, Artie, 106
Shaw, Arvell, 112
Sheehan, Pat, 58
Shilkret, Nat, 123
Silvers, Phil, 110, 193
Sinatra, Frank, 59, 95, 100, 117, 130, 142, 159, 177, 185, 193, 196, 205
Smith, Bessie, 105
Smith, Kate, 33, 117, 146, 187
Sousa, John Philip, 3
Starr, Kay, 110, 113, 201
Strutters, Harry, 200
Sullivan, Ed, 122

T
Taylor, James, 183
Taylor, Tommy, 202
Teagarden, Jack, 16, 102, 106, 111, 112, 123
Teagarden, Charlie, 16, 111, 123
Tormé, Jan, 182
Tormé, Mel, 117, 158, 182, 183
Tracy, Arthur, 192
Tracy, Spencer, 47
Trotter, John Scott, 89, 90, 115, 117, 127-130, 152, 206
Trumbauer, Frank (Tram), 16, 102, 106, 107, 112, 123
Trump, Donald, 197
Turner, Ray, 15, 122
Twiss, Ken, 203

V
Vale, Jerry, 158, 185, 193, 196
Vallee, Rudy, 68, 69, 186
Van Heusen, James, 60, 138, 139, 141, 142, 204
Venuti, Joe, 102, 105, 106, 108, 112, 113, 123, 170, 179

W
Wallichs, Glen, 133
Waring, Fred, 117, 170
Wayne, John, 86, 98, 201
Weeks, Anson, 39, 105
Weems, Ted, 197
Weissmuller, Johnny, 68
Welch, Raquel, 59
Whiteman, Paul, 11, 13-16, 18, 19, 25, 102, 106, 111, 113, 122, 123, 125, 159, 166, 168, 179, 185
Whiting, Margaret, 144
Whiting, Richard, 144
Whitney, Jock, 62
Wiggins, F.B. (Wig), 120
Winfrey, Oprah, 197
Williams, Andy, 117.
Williams Brothers, The, 117
Wilson, John S., 126
Winninger, Charles, 153
Wirz, Max, 198-205

Y
Young, Victor, 117

CELEBRITY PROFILES PUBLISHING
BOX 344 Main Street
STONY BROOK, NY 11790

(631) 862-8555 • FAX (631) 862-0139 • e-mail: celebpro4@aol.com

The BEST DAMN TRUMPET PLAYER   Copies _____
ISBN 1-57579-011-4   196 Pages   55 Photos
Price $15.95
****

The SONG STARS   Copies _____
ISBN 1-57579-045-9   240 Pages   60 Photos
Price $17.95
****

The MUSIC MEN   Copies _____
ISBN 1-57579-097-1   250 Pages   70 Photos
PRICE $17.95
****

JUKEBOX SATURDAY NIGHT   Copies_____
ISBN 1-57579-142-0   250 Pages   70 Photos
PRICE $17.95
****

SNOOTIE LITTLE CUTIE — The Connie Haines Story   Copies_____
ISBN 1-57579-143-9   144 Pages   77 Photos
PRICE $17.95
****

JERRY VALE — A Singer's Life   Copies_____
ISBN 1-57579-176-5   216 Pages   117 Photos
PRICE $19.95

****

THE SPIRIT OF BOB HOPE —
One Hundred Years, One Million Laughs   Copies_____
ISBN 1-57579-227-3   208 Pages   132 Photos
PRICE $19.95

****

BING CROSBY —
Crooner of the Century   Copies_____
ISBN 1-57579-248-6   272 Pages   171 Photos
PRICE $19.95
****

NAME _____

ADDRESS_____

CITY, TOWN, STATE_____ ZIP CODE_____

Include $3.50 for Priority Mail (2 days arrival time) for up to 2 books.
Enclose check or money order. Order will be shipped immediately.

For CREDIT CARDS, please fill out as shown below:

Card #_____ Exp. Date_____

Signature_____

VISA ___AMEX ___ DISCOVER___MASTER CARD___(CHECK ONE)